22.95

INTERIM SITE

The Ocean Book

The Ocean Book

Aquarium and Seaside Activities and Ideas for All Ages

Center for Marine Conservation

WILEY

John Wiley & Sons, Inc.

New York • Chichester • Brisbane • Toronto • Singapore

PUBLISHER: Stephen Kippur
EDITOR: David Sobel
MANAGING EDITOR: Corinne McCormick
COMPOSITION: Folio Graphics Company, Inc.
PROJECT DIRECTOR: Linda Maraniss
CMC ART DIRECTOR AND ILLUSTRATOR: Jill Perry Townsend
PROJECT DIRECTOR (SECOND EDITION): Susie Gwen Criswell
CMC STAFF ADVISORS: Natasha Atkins, Rose Bierce, Twig George, Roger McManus, Richard Townsend, Michael Weber
SPECIAL THANKS TO: Isaac Asimov, Scott Carpenter, Thomas Grooms, David Pittenger, Dr. Naida Yolen, Mary E. Kennan

All activities and information presented in *The Ocean Book: Aquarium and Seaside Activities and Ideas for All Ages* are courtesy of the Center for Marine Conservation, unless otherwise noted.

Material from this book may be reproduced for classroom use only. Write for information on other marine educational materials available from the Center for Marine Conservation. This publication is designed to provide accurate and authoritative information in regard to the subject matter covered. It is sold with the understanding that the publisher is not engaged in rendering legal, accounting, or other professional service. If legal advice or other expert assistance is required, the services of a competent professional person should be sought. FROM A DECLARATION OF PRINCIPLES JOINTLY ADOPTED BY A COMMITTEE OF THE AMERICAN BAR ASSOCIATION AND A COMMITTEE OF PUBLISHERS.

Library of Congress Cataloging-in-Publication Data

Center for Marine Conservation

The ocean book: aquarium and seaside activities
and ideas for all ages/ Center for Marine Conservation

ISBN 0471-50973-6
ISBN 0-471-62078-5 (pprbk)

Printed in the United States of America

89 90 10 9 8 7 6 5 4 3 2 1

About the Center for Marine Conservation

The Center for Marine Conservation (formerly the Center for Environmental Education), established in 1972, is a non-profit membership organization dedicated to protecting marine wildlife and their habitats, and to conserving coastal and ocean resources.

The Center is among the world's most respected conservation organizations. With more than 110,000 members nationwide, we work with private industry, other conservation groups, government, and private citizens to protect marine wildlife and keep the marine environment healthy and safe for future generations. Our view is that permanent changes in attitudes and policies can best be achieved through education, cooperation, and understanding.

The Center achieves its objectives by:

- Conducting policy-oriented research
- Promoting public awareness and education
- Involving citizens in public policy decisions
- Supporting domestic and international conservation programs for marine species and their habitats

Headquartered in Washington, D.C., the Center has regional offices in Texas, Florida, Virginia and California.

Center for Marine Conservation
1725 DeSales Street
Suite 500
Washington, D.C. 20036

Acknowledgments

During the Year of the Ocean, celebrated in 1984–85, the Center for Environmental Education (now known as the Center for Marine Conservation), a non-profit marine conservation organization based in Washington, D.C., received funding from the David and Lucile Packard Foundation and the Year of the Ocean Foundation to produce an activity book for children about the ocean. We contacted major aquariums and marine science centers, inviting them to contribute their best educational materials for inclusion in the book along with materials created by the Center. In August 1985, we proudly published *The Ocean: Consider the Connections*. Teachers, parents and students responded so favorably that the book was reprinted two times.

That original book represented the creative efforts of over 25 marine education centers from Hawaii to Massachusetts. We all benefitted from the generous sharing of so many talented organizations.

It is with great pleasure that we now present *The Ocean Book: Aquarium and Seaside Activities and Ideas for All Ages,* a revised and larger version of *Consider the Connections,* and wish to thank John Wiley & Sons for their interest in the topic of marine education and for their desire to publish this expanded edition.

Thanks to:

Atlanta Zoo, Atlanta, GA
Brookfield Zoo, Brookfield, IL
Center for Marine Conservation, Washington, DC
Fort Worth Zoological Park, Fort Worth, TX
Freshwater Society, Navarre, MN
Gladys Porter Zoo, Brownsville, TX
Innovative Communications, Walnut Creek, CA
John G. Shedd Aquarium, Chicago, IL
Los Angeles Zoo, Los Angeles, CA
Marine Resources Development Foundation, Ft. Lauderdale, FL
Marine Science Center, Newport, OR
Marine Science Center, Poulsbo, WA
Minnesota Zoo, Apple Valley, MN
Monterey Bay Aquarium, Monterey, CA
Mystic Marinelife Aquarium, Mystic, CT
National Aquarium in Baltimore, Baltimore, MD
New England Aquarium, Boston, MA
North Carolina Aquarium on Roanoke Island, Manteo, NC
Point Reyes Bird Observatory, Stinson Beach, CA
Riverbanks Zoological Park, Columbia, SC
Scripps Institution of Oceanography, La Jolla, CA
Sea-Arama/ Marineworld, Galveston, TX
Sea Life Park, Waimanalo, HI
Seattle Aquarium, Seattle, WA
Sea World Ohio, Aurora, OH
Sea World San Diego, San Diego, CA
Smithsonian Environmental Center, Edgewater, MD
University of Southern California, Sea Grant Marine Education Program, Los Angeles, CA
U.S. Department of Commerce, Office of Ocean and Coastal Resource Management.
    Washington, DC
Whale Center, Oakland, CA

Contents

Foreword by Isaac Asimov

Our planet, Earth, is the only one in the Solar system that has a vast open ocean of liquid water. Mercury, Venus, and the Moon are all bone-dry. The great outer planets seem to have water as part of their structure but it is lost in mixture with vastly greater quantities of hydrogen and helium.

On the smaller worlds that lie beyond Earth—from Mars outward—any water that is present is in the form of ice. The one possible exception is Jupiter's satellite, Europa, the surface of which is one globe-encircling glacier. Under that glacier there may be liquid water, but it is not an open ocean; it is forever in the dark.

It is Earth's unique ocean that makes our planet uniquely life-bearing. Life began in the ocean perhaps three and a half billion years ago, when Earth was only a billion years old. It has flourished in the ocean ever since.

In fact, the waters of the Earth were the *only* home of life for fully three billion years. Until four hundred million years ago, Earth's dry land was sterile; it bore no life. This means that for nine-tenths of the Earth's existence, there was no life on land.

This is not surprising. Consider the differences of sea and land. The ocean has a temperature which changes very little with the seasons, but land is exposed to extremes of temperature. The water of the ocean screens out the harsh radiation of the Sun, while the air above the land is much less effective in doing this. The water of the ocean is buoyant and lifts up life forms so that they are little affected by gravity and can move easily in three dimensions, no matter how large they are. Life on land is pulled down forcefully by gravity and any animal that weighs more than twenty-five pounds or so can move about rapidly only at the cost of a large expenditure of energy.

Even today the ocean life is far more important in the total scheme of things than land life is. There are microscopic plant cells in the top layer of the ocean, for instance, that produce four times as much oxygen and food as the green plants of the land do. If all land life should disappear, life in the ocean might be handicapped in some minor ways, but it would continue. If all ocean life were to disappear, however, animal life on land could continue only in greatly reduced quantity—if at all.

How important it is for us, then, to conserve ocean life; to keep the ocean waters clean and wholesome; to protect important kinds of ocean life from growing extinct. We must cherish our wonderful, our unique ocean.

All of life on Earth is interconnected and to whatever extent we make it less possible for ocean life to flourish, we make that much less possible for land life and for ourselves to flourish.

Introduction

Many children often consider the worlds' oceans as so distant and awesome, so vast and deep, that they rarely think about their connections to this vital force. The Center for Marine Conservation believes that once a person establishes a relationship or an understanding of an environment, that place will remain special. With over 70% of our planet covered with water it is indeed important that future generations of decision makers are informed about this fragile resource. We believe that the more children know about the oceans, and come to understand them, the more they will care for them and will want to work hard to protect them from pollution or destruction.

A field trip along the rocky coasts of Oregon or Maine, a stroll along the beaches of Florida, Texas, California, or a visit to the Carolinas are some of the best ways possible to establish this bond. Although 50 percent of the people in the U.S. live within 100 miles of a coastline, it is not always easy to arrange a seashore visit. This activity book is a wonderful supplement for those classes and families fortunate enough to travel to the ocean. *The Ocean Book: Aquarium and Seaside Activities and Ideas for All Ages* will help those of us who are "land-locked" as well, by instilling within our children a greater knowledge and sense of respect for our oceans.

Without leaving home or classroom, children can discover the ocean and its creatures by reading, creating art projects, completing word puzzles and conducting science experiments. Each chapter of this resource and activity book begins with background information for adults. Most of the activities are designed for children to complete independently. Teachers will find that the design of the book promotes easy duplication of the activities for classroom use. The final chapter provides answers to the activities, enabling the children to correct themselves or for the book to be used as a teachers' manual.

Chapter One, "Dive In," will help youngsters identify the world's oceans, understand the importance of the water cycle, and become familiar with the ocean floor. Chapter Two, "The Ocean at Work," provides budding oceanographers with experiments to help them understand salinity and temperature currents. Children will also see the effect water has on land temperatures by studying the temperatures of coastal and inland Oregon cities. Tides and waves are explained through art projects. The ocean is home for many unique animals, and Chapter Three, "Who's Who," is full of do-and-learn activities that will teach about whales, seals, sea lions, and one of the most endangered animals in the world, sea turtles. Children will also be introduced to the ancient Japanese art of fish printing.

Many children have learned about food chains involving animals and plants on land. In Chapter Four, "Come and Eat," they will learn about food chains beneath the sea. Chapter Five deals with the interesting topic of adaptation and how color, shape, and behavior patterns are the key to survival. Have the crayons ready as the subjects of camouflage, coloration and partnerships are explored.

The beauty of tidepools, beaches and coral reefs are the highlight of "Ecosystems" in Chapter Six. Children can design a beach and an estuary of their choice with the information provided and additional research. A special 'at the beach' activity is presented as well as useful information on how to keep a log on beach visits. Chapter Seven, "People and the Sea," introduces children to several people who have made the marine world part of their lives. Chapter Eight offers a handy reference section with a vocabulary and book list, providing useful information to those who want to learn more. The answers to most of the investigative activities will be found in this final chapter.

The Center for Marine Conservation believes that the marine environment is a fascinating topic to introduce to young people, whether it be in relation to creative writing, math, art, science, or language skills. The aquariums, beaches, marshes, all of the coastal areas of this country need the support and concern of our young people. Instilling this concern and support in children is a great challenge to parents and teachers. Take this book into your classrooms and homes and introduce children to the ocean; everyone can then explore the shore with a greater sense of interest.

Dive In: The Beginning of Your Ocean Study

Photos taken from outer space show Earth to be a beautiful blue planet. The blue is water, which covers over 70% of the Earth's surface. The continents we live on are simply large islands set in the ocean. Although maps show oceans with separate names, it is important to remember that the ocean is one body of water. This abundance of water makes life possible and therefore makes Earth different from all other planets.

Most of us live within a few hundred miles of the ocean and yet know very little about the marine environment. While adults relax at the beach, it is often the small child playing nearby who reveals a natural curiosity about the ocean. Many of their questions are similar to the ones asked by mankind for centuries. Why is the ocean blue? What makes the waves? What lives in the ocean? Why is the ocean salty? How deep is the ocean?

The search for answers to these and thousands of other questions about the ocean has led to scientific exploration at and below the water's surface. Information provided by marine scientists has made us aware of the importance of the sea to our survival, as well as the survival of the plants and animals that live on land and in the sea.

The ocean is fascinating, complex, and fragile. In order to protect it we must understand it. We hope that this section of *The Ocean Book* will be the beginning of a lifelong interest in the sea and its protection. And now, DIVE IN!

Activities in This Chapter

World Map to Color and Label
Use a globe or world map to help you complete this activity.

Water Cycle
Most of the water that falls to earth is evaporated ocean water. Read about and color this water cycle drawing.

The Water Cycle, a crossword puzzle
Complete this puzzle with help from the words provided in the activity.

The Ocean Floor
Identify the parts of the ocean floor.

Gee Whiz Ocean Quiz
How much do you know about the ocean?

"Fish"—a card game
Fun and review during the study of the ocean.

World Map to Color and Label

Did you know the Earth's surface is over 70% water? The ocean holds 97% of the world's water. Two percent is ice in the polar icecaps, and only one percent is fresh water. Study the map below. Label all the oceans. Use a globe or world map to find the names you do not know. Color the oceans blue. Color the land brown.

Use the following list of oceans for help:

Atlantic Ocean
Pacific Ocean
Arctic Ocean
Indian Ocean
Southern (Antarctic) Ocean

What is the biggest ocean?

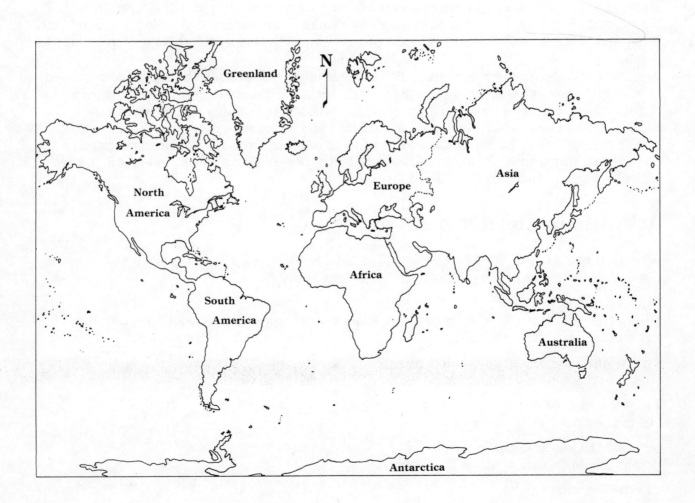

Water Cycle

Water goes around in a cycle. It goes from the sky, to earth, to rivers, to oceans, and back to the sky again. Follow the snow and rain and make RED arrows tracing its cycle back to the clouds. Afterward, color the picture.

4. When the water vapor gets heavy, it falls back to the ground. If it is cold, it falls as snow. If it is warm, it falls as rain.

3. This gas is called **Water Vapor.** It rises and forms clouds.

1. **Precipitation** happens when rain, snow, sleet, or hail falls to the earth from the clouds. Some of the water soaks into the ground. The rest flows into streams, lakes, and oceans.

2. **Evaporation** happens when the sun warms the water and changes some of it into a gas.

The Water Cycle
a crossword puzzle

Where does the water come from that fills Maryland's mountain streams and flows to the Atlantic Ocean? Water is constantly circulating in a sun-powered system in which water evaporates from the ocean and land and returns to the earth as (14) _____. A word you might hear on the evening weather report for rain or snow or sleet is (15) _____.

Some of the water that reaches the earth is immediately taken up by plants. Some of it turns to vapor and forms clouds. This is called (6) _____. Most water falls on the ground and finds its way to small (5) _____ which flow into (1) _____. The water that flows across the ground and into streams is called (8) _____. It often carries soil and decayed materials into the streams. Some water filters directly onto the ground. Water flowing under the earth is called (10) _____. The (4 down) _____ is a measure of how close the water is to the surface of the ground.

Water changes as it flows from streams and rivers to the (13) _____. You can taste the difference in the (2) _____ of the water. Water in mountain streams tastes (11) _____. Water from the ocean tastes like (9) _____. When the water table is at or near the surface of the ground (4 across) _____ are formed. Some are fresh water and some are a combination of fresh and salt water called (3) _____ water. A wetland area with brackish water is called a salt (7) _____. An area like the Chesapeake Bay where fresh water from rivers and salt water from the ocean mix is called an (12) _____.

Waters from the Chesapeake Bay eventually flow into the Atlantic Ocean. What happens to the water after it reaches the ocean? Heat from the sun causes it to evaporate and the water (16) _____ begins all over again.

WORDS USED IN THIS PUZZLE

brackish	fresh	rivers	water table
cycle	marsh	runoff	wetlands
estuary	ocean	salinity	
evaporation	precipitation	streams	
salt	rain	groundwater	

The Water Cycle

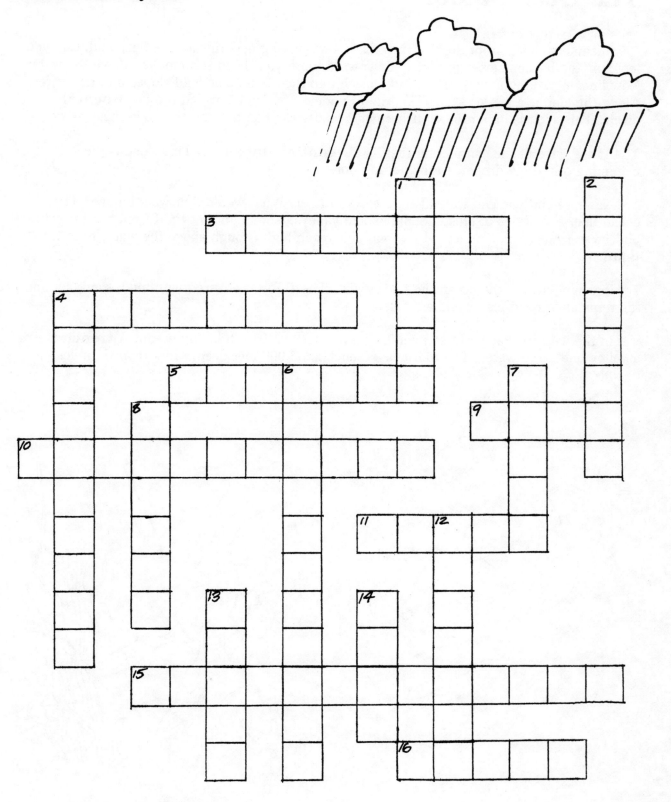

Courtesy of National Aquarium in Baltimore

The Ocean Floor

Imagine walking from the shallow end of a swimming pool toward the deep end. Can you feel how the bottom slopes gradually downward, until your head is no longer above the water? Now imagine taking a walk off a sandy beach into the ocean. The land slopes into the water. Along the land is a rim or shelf. This rim of underwater land is called the **continental shelf**. This shelf is important to fishermen because the fish they catch live in these areas.

At the edge of the continental shelf is the **continental slope**. This slope is the beginning of the big dropoff to the ocean floor.

Now pretend you can walk along the ocean floor. What would that walk be like? The ocean floor is a series of hills, mountains and valleys. You might get tired from climbing these underwater hills. Some underwater mountains reach high enough above the water to form **islands**.

In some parts of the ocean the floor is flat. The **floor** is covered with mud, sand, silt and the remains of dead plants and animals.

In the western Pacific Ocean you'll find the deepest trench in any ocean. A **trench** is like a valley under the water. The Marianas Trench is 35,000 feet deep. More than six miles down!

The Ocean Floor

After reading the page on the parts of the ocean floor, put the correct number in the circle next to the picture of the ocean floor described below.

1. **Continental shelf**: This area rims the land, and is important to fishermen because of the fish that live in the shallow waters above the shelf.

2. **Continental slope**: The big dropoff to the ocean floor.

3. **Trench**: A valley under the water.

4. **Floor**: Sometimes flat, covered with mud and the remains of dead animals and plants.

5. **Island**: The top of an undersea mountain.

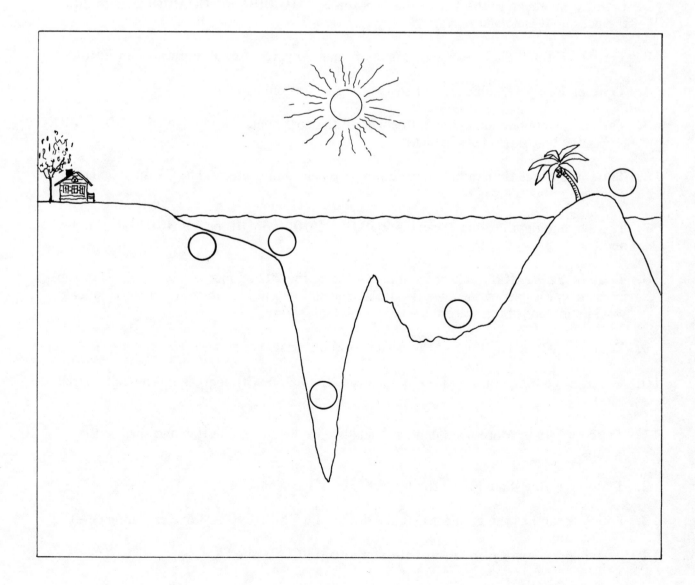

Gee Whiz Ocean Quiz

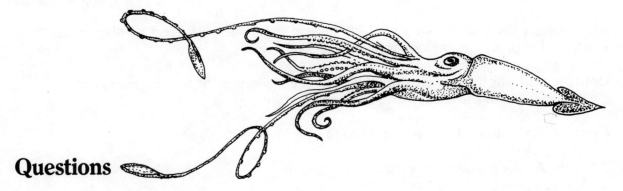

Questions

1. **True** or **False**: The interconnected waters of the oceans cover over 70 percent of the Earth's surface.

2. It would take a river the size of the Amazon **3, 10,000** or **200,000** years to drain the oceans. (Circle one.)

3. **True** or **False**: The ocean contains more than 90 percent of all the water on Earth.

4. **True** or **False**: A cubic mile of sea water contains only water.

5. The oceans contain enough salt to cover all the continents with a layer **5, 50, 500** or **5,000** feet thick. (Circle one.)

6. **True** or **False**: Human blood, excluding the cells and proteins, has the same general composition as sea water.

7. The average depth of the oceans is **200, 1,200, 6,400** or **12,300** feet. (Circle one.)

8. **True** or **False**: If the tallest mountain on land, the 29,028 foot Mt. Everest, were sunk in the deepest part of the oceans—the Marianas Deep in the western Pacific—its peak would stick out of the water.

9. **True** or **False**: The floor of the oceans off our coasts is flat.

10. The average temperature of the oceans is **23, 38,** or **66** degrees Fahrenheit. (Circle one.)

11. **True** or **False**: More plants and animals live in the air and on the land than in the oceans.

12. **True** or **False**: Squid have the largest eyes of any animal.

13. Which ocean has the greatest average depth: the **Pacific** or **Atlantic**? (Circle one.)

14. Barrel sponges are **plants, animals** or **fungi**. (Circle one.)

15. The largest animal ever to live on Earth is the **blue whale, elephant** or **brontosaurus**. (Circle one.)

16. True or **False**: Crabs release only a few eggs each season.

17. The United States has a tidal shoreline of **26,000,   88,000** or **124,000** miles. (Circle one.)

18. True or **False**: The population of the U.S. is concentrated near the coasts.

19. True or **False**: Recreational saltwater fishing is a popular activity.

20. True or **False**: Lagoons, estuaries and saltwater marshes are not valuable.

21. True or **False**: "Red tides" are caused by the release of chemicals from the ocean floor.

22. True or **False**: The sea has always been at the same level.

23. True or **False**: Sperm whales' teeth grow up to ten inches long and weigh up to four pounds each.

24. True or **False**: Emperor penguins incubate their eggs on their feet.

25. True or **False**: Penguins depend completely on the ocean for food.

26. True or **False**: A newborn baby blue whale weighs more than 2,000 pounds.

27. True or **False**: An adult emperor penguin can be over three feet tall.

28. True or **False**: All the world's oceans are blue.

29. True or **False**: Sea shells in the ocean make the water salty.

30. True or **False**: Some ice in the Arctic Ocean is over 50 feet thick.

"Fish"—a card game

Objectives
The student will try to obtain the most pairs of cards in the card game "FISH."

Start
Deal four cards to each player. In rotating order, one player selects one other player to ask for a card to match the one in his/her hand. If the player does not have the card, he/she tells the "requesting player" to "fish" (to pick a card from the deck). If the player is given the card that was requested, he/she puts the pair face down in front of him/her and is allowed to request another card from another player. As pairs are accumulated and the game has ended, players count their pairs. The player with the most pairs wins.

Materials
Students can make the cards needed; one card has the word on it and the other card has the picture drawn or pasted on it to illustrate the word.

Cards to Match (with pictures)

iceberg	algae	island
Pacific Ocean	wave	shrimp
Indian Ocean	nodules	oysters
Atlantic Ocean	oceanographer	crab
plankton	starfish	squid
volcano	shark	Moby Dick
coral reef	submarine	wet suit
trilobites	jellyfish	eel
nautilus	sea urchin	sea anemone
octopus	diatoms	mussel
beach	kelp	dolphin
whale	manta ray	mid-ocean ridge
clam	Trieste	Marianas Trench
supertanker	seal	sea urchin
harbor	lobster	oil platform
nansen bottle	fisherman	compass
mermaid	sea monster	

Courtesy of the University of Southern California Sea Grant Program

Currents, Weather, Waves and Tides: The Ocean at Work

The ocean is an extremely important climate regulator. In fact, the ocean dominates the world's climate. Most of the water that falls to Earth as rain or snow is evaporated sea water.

Water has unique physical properties which stabilize temperatures on Earth. Water has the ability to absorb heat from the sun without getting too hot and radiate heat without getting too cold. Water can absorb more than five times as much heat as land before changing temperature. Daily land temperatures fluctuate much more than do daily ocean temperatures.

Winds are created by the temperature differences between land and sea. Winds generally rise over the hotter land during the day creating onshore breezes and rise faster over the warmer water at night causing offshore breezes.

Winds cause waves and surface currents. Currents generally form a pattern of closed loops that turn clockwise in the Northern Hemisphere and counter clockwise in the Southern Hemisphere. The major currents tend to follow the pattern of the prevailing winds.

Undersea currents are created by differences in salt content and temperature. Ocean currents transport heat and cold over thousands of miles. Currents carry warm equatorial water toward the poles and cold polar water toward the equator. The Gulf Stream, for instance, carries warm water from the Gulf of Mexico north to Canada and then veers toward Europe. This large moving body of warm water, like a river almost 40 miles wide and 2,000 feet deep, affects the temperature all along the East Coast of the United States, the British Isles and Norway.

The Humbolt Current carries cold water from the polar regions to the western coast of South America. A small change in the temperature of the ocean may affect weather on land. One of the most destructive climatic events in modern history occurred in 1982-1983 with a phenomenon known as El Niño. El Niño replaces normally cold currents with warm currents along the Pacific coasts of South America. This shift in temperature causes an increase of rain to the dry coast of Peru. The heavy rainfall leads to flooding, landslides, crop destruction, and loss of human lives. At sea, this above normal ocean temperature results in death to marine animals, upsetting the food chain from plants to birds to fish to people. The devastating effects of El Niño are felt worldwide.

Experts are still investigating the causes of this event, but many scientists believe that the triggering mechanism for El Niño involves the unstable interactions between the ocean and a low pressure cell in the atmosphere.

Activities in This Chapter

Ocean Currents
These two experiments demonstrate the effects of temperature and salinity on water.

How Does the Ocean Change Our Coastline?
This experiment with sand and water will show how waves shape a beach. You will need a few days to prepare this experiment.

Tides and a Tide Mobile
Make this tide mobile to illustrate Spring and Neap Tides.

Making Waves
Identify and draw the parts of a wave.

The Ocean? No Sweat!
Complete this activity to see what effect the ocean has on the temperatures of different cities. You will need an Atlas with the state of Oregon for reference.

Ocean Currents

Teachers: Read this before you start experiments

While this experiment can be done as a demonstration, it is recommended that the class be divided into small groups and that each group perform the investigations. This exercise deals with temperature and salinity currents. Emphasize that currents do exist and that they play an important and not all together understood role in the life of the oceans.

Duplicate the materials. One set per student. It is important that you do this experiment before your class performs it. This will give you a chance to anticipate any difficulties. Try the 3 x 5 card on the top of the flask inversion trick for yourself. It really does work. Be sure your flasks or jars have flat lips.

Groups of 3 or 4 students allow participation by all members. Watch to see that some don't adopt a passive spectator role.

Encourage careful observation and require written observations from the groups.

Ocean Currents

People have observed ocean *currents* for many years. Currents are masses of water that flow in a definite direction. Ocean currents are important in many ways. They affect the climate of the lands nearby. The best fishing is often found where two currents come together. Currents can help *transport* boats. They also transport fish and shellfish that are too young to swim great distances.

There are several types of currents. The best known are wind-caused currents where the wind actually pushes the water along the surface. There are also deep currents beneath the surface. These currents are caused mainly by differences in the *density* of *adjacent* waters.

The experiment below will let you observe two of the lesser known factors that cause currents. You will observe differences in salinity and temperature densities between two masses of water.

Materials

Two 1-pint milk bottles or two 250 milliliter Erlenmeyer flasks with flat rims
Some 3 x 5 cards
Table salt
Food coloring
Paper towels or rags
Plastic dishpan or other container suitable to catch water

Experiment 1: Salinity Currents

Method

1. Fill both bottles with water. Dissolve ½ teaspoon of salt in one bottle and add a drop of food coloring. Place a 3 x 5 card on top of the salt water bottle and carefully invert it; the upward pressure of air will hold the card in place (most of the time).

a. Place the salt water bottle on top of the fresh water container and have someone remove the card. (Now is the time for the dish pan!) Observe results.
b. Repeat No. 1—place fresh water jar on top of salt water jar, remove card and observe.
c. Repeat No. 1—place both jars horizontally, remove card and observe.

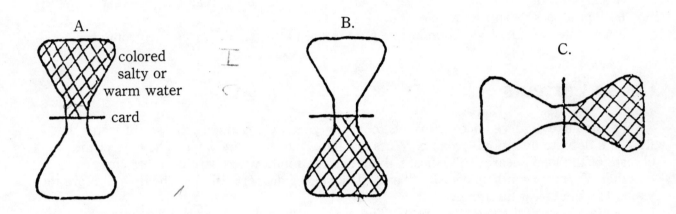

Interpretation

1. Is salt water heavier or lighter (higher or lower density) than fresh water? Explain your answer in terms of the results you obtained from the experiment.
2. What happens to river water when it flows into the ocean?
3. Freddy Fisherman was fishing at a spot near the *mouth* of a river. Five feet down he caught a fresh water perch. His luck was so good he let out more line. At thirty feet he caught a salt water cod. Freddy is so excited about this strange occurrence he is going to call the Sports Editor of the Post-Intelligencer. What would you tell Freddy to save him from embarassment?

Experiment 2: Temperature Currents

Method

2. Fill one bottle with warm water and the other with cool water. Add a drop of food coloring to the warm water. Do the three variations listed in Experiment No. 1. (see diagram below).

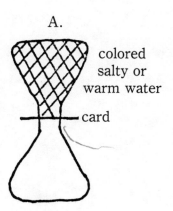 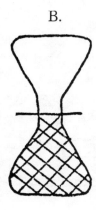 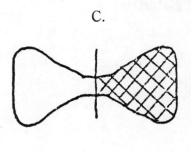

A.

colored
salty or
warm water

card

B.

C.

Interpretation

1. Is warm water heavier or lighter (higher or lower density) than cool water? Explain your answer in terms of the results you obtained on the above experiment.
2. Where does most heating of ocean water take place?
3. Where does most dilution of sea water occur?
4. Is it easier for a human to swim in salty or in fresh water? Explain.
5. Is it easier for a human to swim in cool water or warm water? Explain.

How Does the Ocean Change Our Coastline?

Objective

Given the appropriate materials, the children will demonstrate how waves break and how the action of waves can shape a beach.

Materials

Dish pan, board, soil, sand, and water. Diagram:

Procedure

See diagram above. Put board in pan about 5″ from one end. The board should be about as high as the rim of the pan. Fill 5″ side with soil and wet it until it is a paste-like mud. Tap it down solidly and **let it dry for a few days**.

After the soil has dried, put 2″ of sand in the pan on the other side of the board. Add about 1½″ of water above the sand. Remove the board. Move the board back and forth in the water until you make small waves. Observe the waves as they erode the soil.

Questions

What happened to the sand as the water washed against one side of it? What relationship does this have to what happens on the beach? Does the sand on the beach also shift? (Perhaps some students have built a sand castle and watched the waves remove it.) Do larger waves make the sand move farther? How do you think the incoming tide affects the movement of the sand?

Explanation

As the energy of the waves is dissipated on the shore, the land is eroded, ultimately making a sloping beach. The reason the waves break is that the drag of the wave motion, as it reaches shallow water, causes the wave to tumble over itself, much as a person ice skating would fall forward when skating off the ice onto dry ground.

As an additional experiment to show that waves do not move water as they travel across the sea, put a small cork on the surface of the water and create waves gently by moving the board as before. Notice that the cork does not move forward as the wave advances. Instead it merely moves up and down or actually in a circular manner as the waves pass by. Thus, waves do not move water across the sea. They are only a surface phenomenon, and it is only when the waves break on the shore that the water particles move back and forth.

Courtesy of the University of Southern California Sea Grant Program

Tides

Tides move the entire ocean. If you have ever been to a beach, you have seen the water come high up on the shore and at other times the water has been much lower. You may have heard people say that the tide is coming in, (high tide) or that it is going out (low tide). This alternate rise and fall of the ocean is called the tide, but what causes the tide?

Tides are caused by the gravitational pull between the Earth, Sun and the Moon. As the Moon rotates around the Earth the water follows it and forms the daily tides. The Sun's effect on the tides is about half that of the Moon's because the Sun is so far from the Earth.

Spring tides are caused when the full Moon (and again with the new Moon) lines up in a straight path with the Sun and the Earth. When the Moon and Sun are in line with the Earth they work together as a tidal team. Spring tides, which occur twice a month all year, rise higher and fall lower than normal.

Neap tides are caused when the Sun, the Earth and the Moon, in the first and third quarters, are at right angles to each other. These tides are unusually low because the pull of the Moon and the pull of the Sun somewhat cancel each other out. The Moon and the Sun engage in a tidal tug of war. Neap tides have the smallest difference between the water levels at high tide and low tide.

Tide Mobile

Materials: one hanger, two sticks, string, magic markers or paint, glue, paper clips.

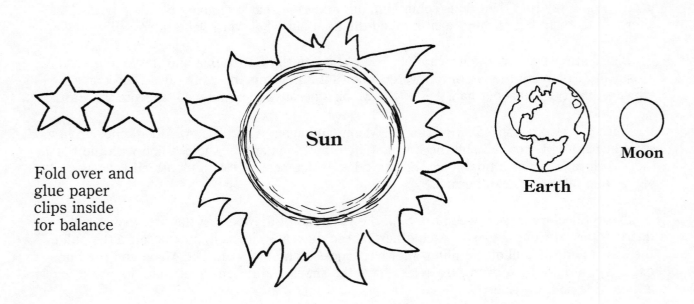

Fold over and glue paper clips inside for balance

On a piece of construction paper draw your own stars, Sun, Earth and Moon. Color or paint the Sun yellow, the Moon purple, Earth blue and green, and the star white.

Construct the mobile like this:

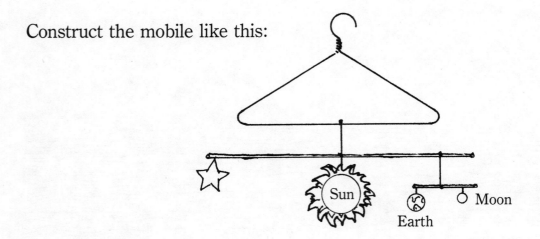

1. What is the position of the Earth, Moon and Sun during Spring Tides?

2. What is the position of the Earth, Moon and Sun during Neap Tides?

Making Waves

All waves have several features in common. They have height, which is the distance from the trough to the crest, they have length, the distance from crest to crest, and all waves move. What creates a wave? The Wind.

In the space below draw your own wave with two crests like this: 〜〜

1. Label the two highest parts of the wave the "CREST."

2. Label the lowest part of the wave the "TROUGH."

3. Figure out the height of your wave (distance from trough to crest)
   if one inch equals ten feet. _____

4. What is the length of your wave (distance from crest to crest) if one inch equals eight feet?
   _____

5. Draw an arrow to show which way the wind is blowing your wave.

The highest wave ever recorded was 112 feet by U.S.S. Rampo, on February 7, 1933.

What other kinds of waves have you heard about but can not see? _____

_____

_____

The Ocean? No Sweat!
How the Oceans Affect Temperatures

Action

On a map of Oregon, have the students locate and label the cities in the list below. They should then subtract the minimum temperatures from the maximum temperatures to find the temperature range and enter it on the map. Have the students analyze the temperature ranges they have written on the map by asking the following questions:

1. Where are the ranges the smallest?
2. Where are the ranges the largest?
3. What do you think are the reasons for this difference?

Data: Minimum and Maximum Temperatures for Some Cities in Oregon in July (C°)*

City	Minimum Temp	Maximum Temp
Ontario	14	35
Burns	12	31
La Grande	12	31
Bend	7	28
Eugene	10	28
Medford	13	32
Salem	10	27
Portland	14	27
Astoria	12	21
North Bend	12	18

*Temperature Data from *Atlas of Oregon* by Loy, Allan, Patton and Plank, U. of O. Books, Eugene, OR, 1976.

Supplemental Activity

Try heating a cup of water and a cup of soil from above with a lamp. Investigate which one will heat up or cool off faster. Have the students predict what will happen.

WASHINGTON

PACIFIC
OCEAN

OREGON

CALIFORNIA

CLATSOP
COLUMBIA
TILLA MOOK
WASHINGTON
MULTNOMAH
HOOD RIVER
YAMHILL
CLACKAMAS
SHER MAN
GILLIAM
MORROW
UMATILLA
UNION
WALLOWA
POLK
MARION
WASCO
LINCOLN
BENTON
LINN
JEFFERSON
WHEELER
BAKER
GRANT
CROOK
COOS
LANE
DESCHUTES
DOUGLAS
CURRY
JOSEPHINE
JACKSON
KLAMATH
LAKE
HARNEY
MALHEUR

CHAPTER 3

Who's Who: Animals in the Ocean

Long ago finding a sunken box of gold coins was a deep sea treasure, but today people realize that the sea itself is a treasure, full of life to discover. Most scientists believe that life began in the sea, and that over billions of years, millions of different organisms have evolved. Animals that now live on land are thought to have developed from those that lived in the ocean. Some ocean animals, such as whales, probably developed from land animals long ago. A tremendous variety of life flourishes in the sea. In fact it is estimated that nine out of every ten organisms on Earth live in the ocean.

The ocean supports life from the microscopic to the gigantic. Tiny one-celled plants floating on the ocean's surface provide the basis for the web of life for water and land animals by making food from the Sun's energy. This process is called photosynthesis. Other plants in the ocean include seaweed and seagrass. Animal life in the ocean can be divided into two categories: vertebrates, animals with backbones, and invertebrates, animals without backbones. Invertebrates include animals like oysters, crabs, periwinkles, jellyfish and the octopus. The octopus is believed to be the most intelligent of the invertebrates.

Vertebrates include all fishes, sea turtles and marine mammals. The fish in the sea delight the imagination with a variety of colors, shapes and life styles. Sea turtles are reptiles that swim the oceans. The female sea turtle only leaves the ocean to crawl on shore to lay her eggs in a sandy nest. Seals are marine mammals that inhabit all the world's oceans, from the polar areas of Antarctica and Alaska to the beaches of Hawaii. The ocean is also home for the whales, the largest creatures to live on this planet. Scientists have been fascinated by the highly developed communication systems used by these mammals. In the future humans hope to understand more about the clicks, whistles and songs emitted by the giants of the sea.

To learn more about the creatures of the ocean, plan a trip to an aquarium. This is a good place to get a close look at marine animals. In this section of *The Ocean Book* you will learn about who's who in the sea from fish to mammals. Have fun!

Activities in This Chapter

Whales and Fish
Complete the chart about two very different ocean animals.

The Order Called Cetacea
Learn about the wide variety of whales and their sizes.

A Whale of a Tail
Fill in the secret message as you learn more about whales.

Body Parts Puzzle
Use this puzzle to learn the body parts of the orca, or killer whales.

The Sounds of Whales
Whales have a highly developed communication system. Try these four listening games for fun.

Marine Mammal Crossword Puzzle
Whales, seals and sea lions are all marine mammals. Learn more about them with this puzzle.

Sea Turtles
Have fun coloring the sea turtles!

Haida the Whale
A true story about a whale and a scientist.

Sharks, Sharks, Sharks
Fun facts about sharks.

Sherlock Shark
Learn the body parts of a shark while you read some fun facts about this sea creature.

Japanese Fish Printing
Gyotaku, the art of Japanese fish printing, will not only provide a hands on study of fish anatomy, but also provides the chance to learn an art form over a century year old.

Invertebrates
Color the invertebrates and see how many you can find in the mangrove swamp.

Ocean Fun
Have fun and learn more about the ocean animals.

Whales and Fish

After you study the picture below, draw lines from the descriptions to the correct animal, either a fish or a whale.

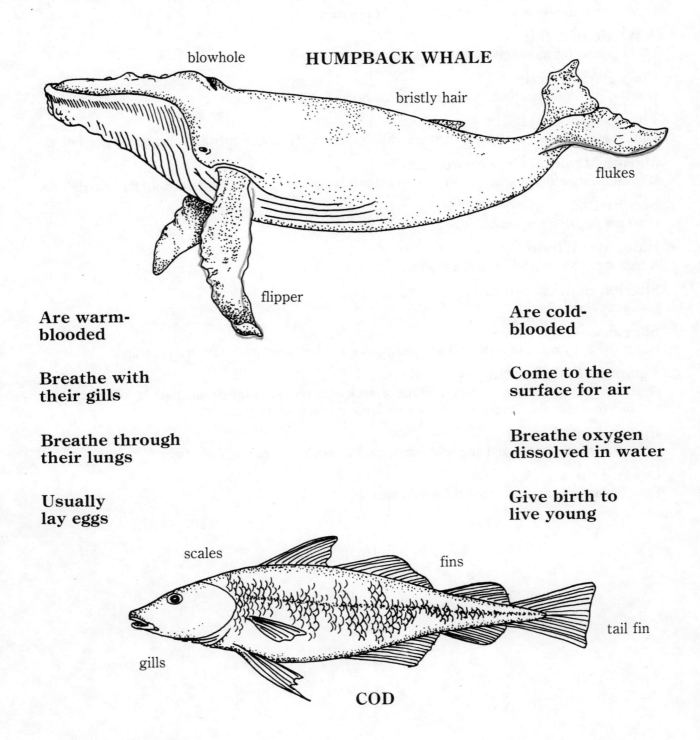

Are warm-blooded

Breathe with their gills

Breathe through their lungs

Usually lay eggs

Are cold-blooded

Come to the surface for air

Breathe oxygen dissolved in water

Give birth to live young

The Order Called Cetacea

Which whales are bigger than your school bus? Take the information from this page and do some drawings of whales. On a large flat surface, such as your playground, draw whales the correct size. Use a measuring tape and bright blue or white chalk.

People who study plants and animals put them into big groups because they have certain things in common. These big groups are called Orders. All whales and dolphins belong to the Order Cetacea. The Order is divided into two big families—toothed whales and baleen whales. Here is a chart that shows these big families.

Baleen Whales

Baleen whales have baleen plates in their mouth that strain the water. They eat the tiny fish and shrimp that get caught in the baleen. They are the biggest animals on the planet and travel enormous distances each year to find their food. A baleen whale's mouth looks like this:

Toothed Whales

Toothed whales have teeth in their mouths and hunt for fish and squid. Some toothed whales have very large brains for their body size. They may use their big brains for communication or for hunting and working together. A toothed whale's mouth looks like this:

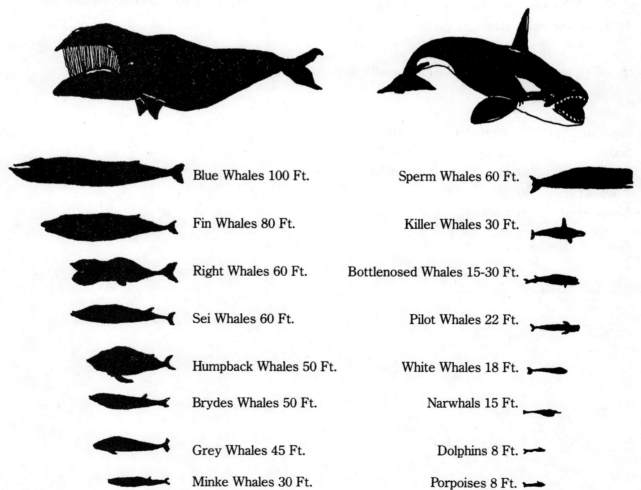

Blue Whales 100 Ft.

Fin Whales 80 Ft.

Right Whales 60 Ft.

Sei Whales 60 Ft.

Humpback Whales 50 Ft.

Brydes Whales 50 Ft.

Grey Whales 45 Ft.

Minke Whales 30 Ft.

Sperm Whales 60 Ft.

Killer Whales 30 Ft.

Bottlenosed Whales 15-30 Ft.

Pilot Whales 22 Ft.

White Whales 18 Ft.

Narwhals 15 Ft.

Dolphins 8 Ft.

Porpoises 8 Ft.

Courtesy of the University of Southern California Sea Grant Program

A Whale of a Tail

Use the words at the bottom of the page to fill in the blanks. You may have to use a word more than once. When you are finished, use the numbered letters to fill in the secret message.

Whales are _ _ _ _ _ _ _ that live in the oceans around the world.
$_{8}$

They have _ _ _ _ _ and breath through their _ _ _ _ _ _ _ _ .
$_{3}$ $_{24}$ $_{2}$ $_{19}$ $_{14}$

They have _ _ _ _ _ _ _ to keep them warm.
$_{11}$

Whales spend all their lives in water.

They are _ _ _ _ _ _ _ animals.
$_{9}$

The two types of whales are _ _ _ _ _ _ _ whales and _ _ _ _ _ _ _ whales.
$_{7}$ $_{5}$

_ _ _ _ _ _ _ whales have _ _ _ _ _ to capture their food of fish and other animals.
$_{15}$ $_{18}$ $_{12}$ $_{16}$

Most _ _ _ _ _ _ whales use their bristle-like hairs to strain small shrimp-like animals, called
$_{21}$

_ _ _ _ _ , from the water.
$_{22}$

In zoos and aquariums, whales learn quickly and are considered to

be _ _ _ _ _ _ _ _ _ _ animals.
$_{17}$ $_{23}$

Some whales use _ _ _ _ _ _ _ _ _ _ _ to find food and also to communicate.
$_{13}$ $_{6}$

Many whales enjoy jumping high above the water. This is called _ _ _ _ _ _ _ _ .
$_{10}$ $_{20}$

A _ _ _ is a group of whales.
$_{4}$ $_{1}$

To spot a whale in the ocean, look for a tall spray of water vapor.

aquatic	**echolocation**	**pod**
baleen	**intelligent**	**teeth**
blowholes	**krill**	**toothed**
blubber	**lungs**	
breaching	**mammals**	

Secret Message:

_ _ _ _ _ _ _ _   _ _ _   _ _ _ _ _ _ _
1 2 3 4 5 6 7 8   9 10 11   12 13 14 15 16 17 18

_ _ _ _ _ _
19 20 21 22 23 24

Courtesy of Shedd Aquarium

Body Parts Puzzle

To learn about the orca, cut out and glue the puzzle pieces to the labeled pattern.

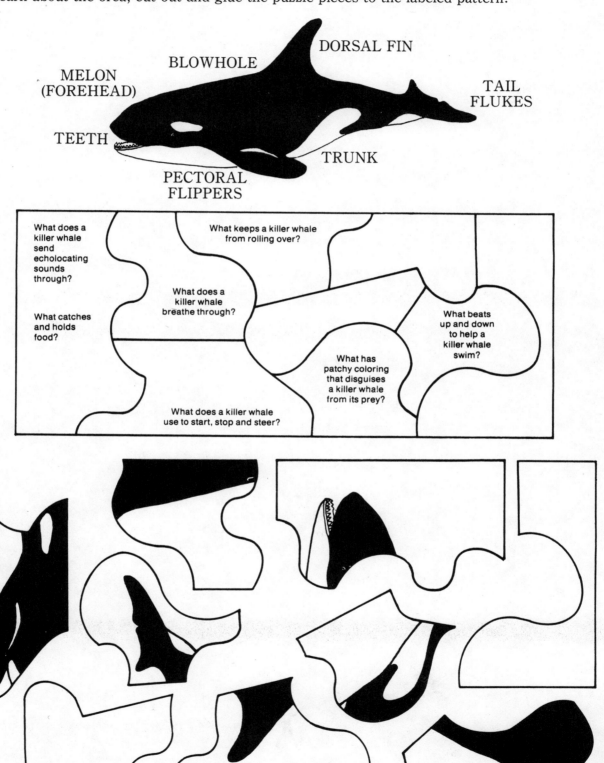

DORSAL FIN

BLOWHOLE

MELON
(FOREHEAD)

TAIL
FLUKES

TEETH

TRUNK

PECTORAL
FLIPPERS

What does a killer whale send echolocating sounds through?

What catches and holds food?

What keeps a killer whale from rolling over?

What does a killer whale breathe through?

What beats up and down to help a killer whale swim?

What has patchy coloring that disguises a killer whale from its prey?

What does a killer whale use to start, stop and steer?

Courtesy of Sea World Ohio

Blank for Cut-out Page

The Sounds of Whales

OBJECTIVES

The students will be able to: 1) increase their skills in auditory discrimination; and 2) identify that whales make a variety of different sounds.

METHOD

Students will identify, respond to, trace and locate various sounds.

MATERIALS NEEDED

A whistle
blindfolds
objects to make various tapping sounds
a recording of whale sounds and
paper and pencils.

PROCEDURE

1) Use a whistle to produce a variety of sounds. Play pairs of notes . . . loud/soft, long/short, high/low. Have the students try to repeat the sounds with their voice. Ask the students to identify and describe the difference between the sounds.
2) Blindfold two children. Ask a third child to walk quietly from one part of the room to another, stopping occasionally to tap objects. After each tapping sound, ask each blindfolded child where the sound's source is. Then ask what object was hit to produce the sound. Are each of them hearing the same thing? Why or why not?
3) Play a recording of whale sounds.* Ask the children to trace with their hands in the air the rise and fall of the whale sounds. Then give them a blank piece of paper and have them record the whale sounds on the paper with a pencil or crayon.
4) Divide the children into groups and choose a leader for each group. Blindfold the other children in the group. Have the leader demonstrate the sound he/she will try to attract their group. Scatter the children and the leaders. Have each group try to locate their leader through the sound the leader produces (clapping, whistle, horn, bell, etc.).

Editor's Note

The ocean is alive with sounds. Whales have a highly developed system of communication. The squeaks, clicks, whistles and cries from whales send messages, find direction and locate food. This is called echolocation. Some whale sounds travel hundreds of miles under water. Scientists study the "songs" of humpback whales and dolphin communication.

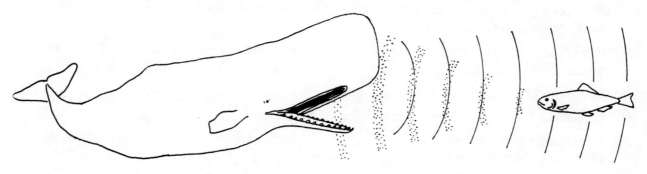

*RECORDS: *Songs of the Humpback Whale,* Roger Payne
              Callings, Paul Winter

Courtesy of Minnesota Zoo

Marine Mammal Crossword Puzzle

ACROSS

1. Some animals can guide themselves with _____ by emitting sound waves into the water which bounce off objects and return to them.

2. Seals, sea lions and walruses belong to a group of marine mammals called_____.

3. Cetaceans travel in small social groups called _____.

4. Most marine mammals have a thick, fatty layer of _____ under the skin to insulate them from the cold.

5. _____ is the term for any animal that eats plants.

6. A pinniped that propels itself with its front flippers and is very agile on land is the _____ _____.

7. The _____ _____ are structures found in female mammals that produce milk to feed the young.

8. One distinguishing characteristic of sea lions is the _____ _____, a small piece of skin that covers the ears.

9. The _____ of the walrus is really an enlarged canine tooth.

10. Like all mammals, whales do have hair in the form of _____ growing on their chins.

11. Cetaceans have a nostril or _____ on top of their heads that is used for breathing.

12. A collective term for tiny plants and animals found floating in the sea is _____.

DOWN

1. A _____ _____ is a furry marine mammal that floats on its back while eating and may even use a rock as a tool.

13. The flattened forelimb of a marine mammal is called the _____.

14. Whales' tails are called _____.

15. A word that describes how whales sometimes leap out of the water and create a big splash is _____.

16. An animal that eats meat is called a _____.

17. A dolphin has a mass of fatty tissue in its forehead called the _____ through which sounds are projected.

18. A pinniped that propels itself with its hind flippers and is generally awkward on land is the _____.

19. Marine mammals, like all mammals, use _____ to breathe.

20. Baleen whales feed on small shrimp-like animals called _____.

21. Marine mammals have very _____ body shapes to cut down on resistance and allow them to move easily through the water.

22. Instead of teeth, some whales feed with sheets of fringed, horny material called_____.

23. Whales and dolphins belong to the group of marine mammals called _____.

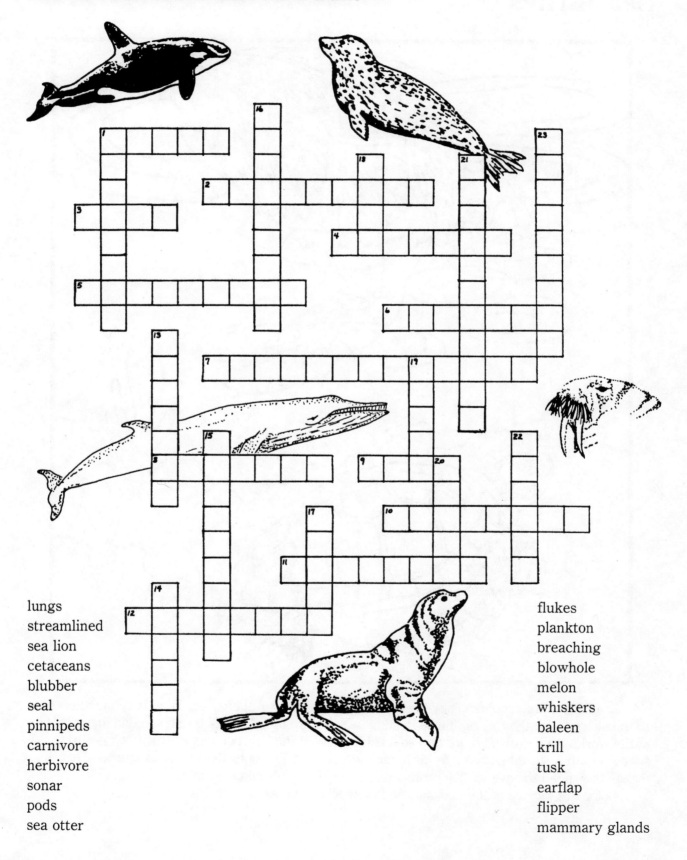

Marine Mammal Crossword Puzzle

lungs
streamlined
sea lion
cetaceans
blubber
seal
pinnipeds
carnivore
herbivore
sonar
pods
sea otter

flukes
plankton
breaching
blowhole
melon
whiskers
baleen
krill
tusk
earflap
flipper
mammary glands

Courtesy of National Aquarium in Baltimore

Sea Turtles

Sea turtles are reptiles. They spend most of their lives in the ocean. Female sea turtles come to the shore to lay their eggs. Turtle nesting beaches are found in this country and in many parts of the world. As more and more people build houses on the beaches and eat turtle eggs, these special creatures are becoming fewer in number. Almost all sea turtles are endangered. That means they need to have special protection so they do not become extinct.

Color this picture of the endangered hawksbill and green sea turtles.

Artwork Courtesy of Shedd Aquarium

This is the True Story of Haida, the Whale Who Taught the Scientist

Dr. Paul Spong is a scientist who studies killer whales. A few years ago, he was working with Haida, a captive killer whale in the Vancouver Aquarium. Dr. Spong and Haida had been doing a lot of different tests, and Dr. Spong was sitting on the edge of the aquarium tank, dangling his bare feet in the water.

Suddenly, without warning, Haida came towards him very fast and opened her awesome mouth. She sliced her teeth across his bare feet just hard enough for him to feel it. Dr. Spong pulled his feet out of the water as soon as he felt Haida's teeth, but if she had really wanted to bite him it would have been too late.

After a while Dr. Spong decided it was safe to put his feet back in the water. Haida came over and did a few more tests with Dr. Spong. Again, without warning, she sliced her teeth across his feet. Again he pulled his feet out of the water, and again he waited for a while before putting his feet back in the water.

Dr. Spong and Haida did this same thing with each other twelve times. By the twelfth time, Dr. Spong knew that Haida wasn't going to hurt his feet, and he left them in the water when she did it again. After that, she never pretended to bite his feet again. Dr. Spong realized that she had been teaching him not to be afraid. Dr. Spong says that killer whales may be the only animals in the world that are not afraid of anything. And one of the most important things they taught him was not to be afraid of them.

Courtesy of the University of Southern California Sea Grant Program

Sharks, Sharks, Sharks

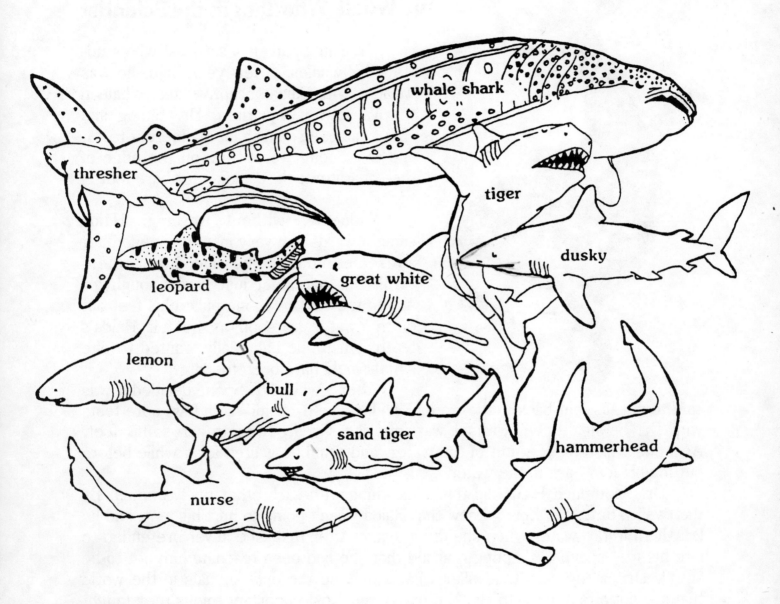

Did you know...

.... that there are about 250 different kinds of sharks?

.... sharks are considered the first living creatures to develop teeth?

.... that many kinds of sharks are afraid of people?

.... that sharks were around three hundred million years ago?

There are many fascinating facts about sharks. Color the sharks and write a report on the kind you find the most interesting.

Sherlock Shark

Decode a Secret Message:

Use the code written below the shark to identify and label the parts of the shark.

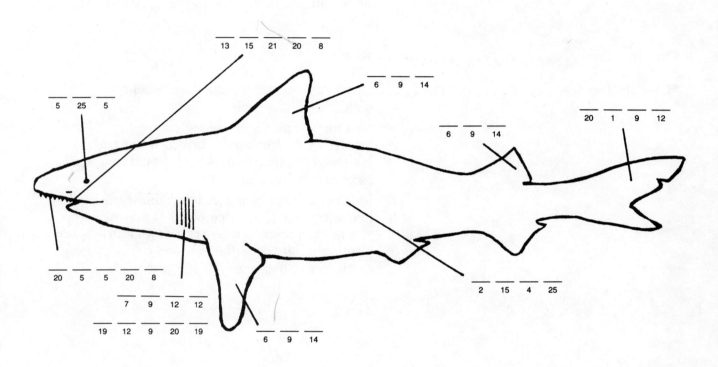

13 15 21 20 8

6 9 14

5 25 5

20 1 9 12

6 9 14

20 5 5 20 8

2 15 4 25

7 9 12 12

19 12 9 20 19

6 9 14

1.	a	7.	g	13.	m	19.	s	25.	y
2.	b	8.	h	14.	n	20.	t	26.	z
3.	c	9.	i	15.	o	21.	u		
4.	d	10.	j	16.	p	22.	v		
5.	e	11.	k	17.	q	23.	w		
6.	f	12.	l	18.	r	24.	x		

What kind of animal is a shark? __ __ __ __
6 9 19 8

GYOTAKU
Japanese Fish Printing

Marine Education Concept . . . . People depend on water for inspiration. Water inspires creative works.

Course Goal . . . . The student will be able to use art materials to show pattern, symmetry and morphology of fish.

Time Required . . . . 40 min.

Materials Required . . . . Fresh or frozen fish (flounders, bluegills, rockfishes work well)

Newspaper, plastic modeling clay, pins, ½″ stiff bristle brush, small paint brush, water-based ink (linoleum block ink is best, liquid tempera paint can be substituted)

Rice paper, newsprint, or other moisture-tolerant paper (since rice paper is expensive you might prefer to start with newsprint; printing on the classified ads can be aesthetically pleasing)

Action

The art of gyotaku (pronounced ghio-ta'-koo) has been used in Japan for more than a century to record catches of sportfish. The Japanese fish printing technique has provided information in ichthyological studies. Scientists at the University of Washington have used fish prints to study the relationship between fish physiology and surface area.

Gyotaku is an excellent interdisciplinary marine education activity. Fish printing can provide an understanding of and appreciation for the beauty and diversity of marine organisms.

1. Use soap and water to clean the outside of the fish as completely as possible. The cleaner the fish, the better the print. Dry the fish well.
2. Place the fish on a table covered with newspapers. Spread the fins out over some clay and pin them in this position. Allow the fish to dry further.
3. Brush on a *thin*, even coat of ink. Leave the eye blank.
4. Paint around the insertion of the pelvic fin leaving a small space between the body and the fin. Paint the pelvic fin.
5. Carefully place a piece of rice paper or newsprint over the inked fish. Use your fingers to gently press the paper over the surface of the fish. Be careful not to change the position of the paper or a double impression will result.
6. Remove the paper from the fish quickly, lifting up one end and peeling it off quickly.
7. Use a small brush to paint the eye.
8. Dry and iron face down (optional).
9. Label your specimens and display them. You may also make prints of shells, flowers, leaves and rocks in this manner.

Questions to Think About

What are some of the characteristics that all fish possess? (Fins, gills, tail fin, and most have scales.)

What are some characteristics that distinguish them from each other?

What does the tail help a fish do? Fins? Gills? Can you find these?

What is the surface area of the fish?

What use could we make of these prints?

How would they help others learn about fish?

Courtesy of Marine Science Center, Newport, OR

Invertebrates

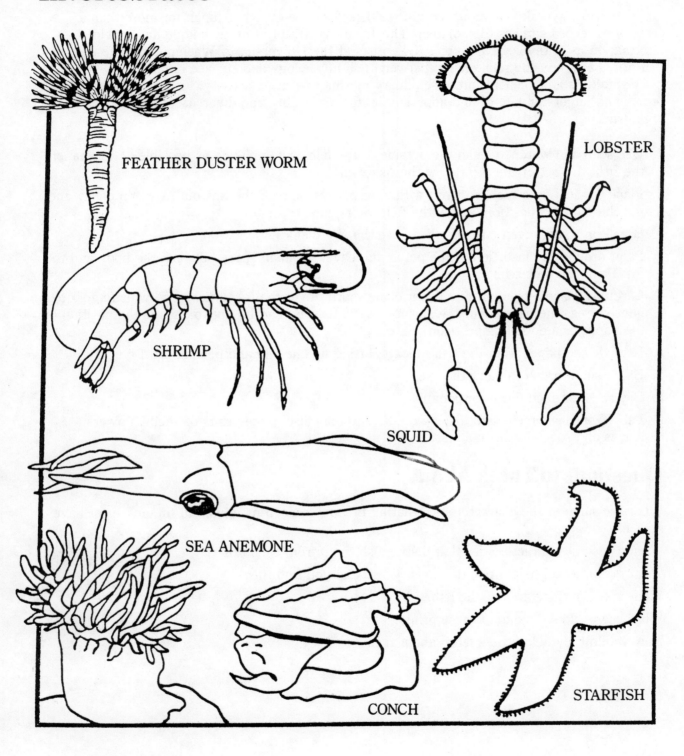

FEATHER DUSTER WORM

LOBSTER

SHRIMP

SQUID

SEA ANEMONE

CONCH

STARFISH

Fish, reptiles and mammals all have backbones. Some animals do not. They are called invertebrates. Color the invertebrates bright, colorful colors.

Artwork Courtesy of Shedd Aquarium

Find Me

Can you find the invertebrates hiding in this mangrove swamp? Color the hidden:

ANEMONE   OCTOPUS   CRAB   OLIVE SHELL

Artwork Courtesy of Shedd Aquarium

Ocean Fun

Language Arts—Ocean Alphabet

Two or more students may play. The first person names a fish. The second person must now name a fish whose name begins with the last letter of the previous name given. For example, 1st person—"sailfish" (H); 2nd person—"halibut" (T); 3rd person—"tuna" (A); etc. If a name cannot be found that begins with a certain letter, that person is eliminated and the next person begins the game with another name. No name may be repeated. Variation: This may encompass *all* forms of marine life including marine mammals, invertebrates, marine plants, etc.

Fishy Riddles

Many ocean creatures have names that are the same as land animals or other objects. The students could play a game by choosing one animal and illustrating it in cartoon style. For example, draw a nurse shark cartoon by drawing a nurse's cap on a shark. Have other students see if they can guess the animal's name. Some good animals for fishy riddles can be seen in our aquarium. They are:

Sea Horse	Hogfish	Leopard Shark
Nurse Shark	Starfish	Turkeyfish
Feather Duster	Angelfish	Stonefish
Sheepshead	Fan Coral	Horseshoe Crab

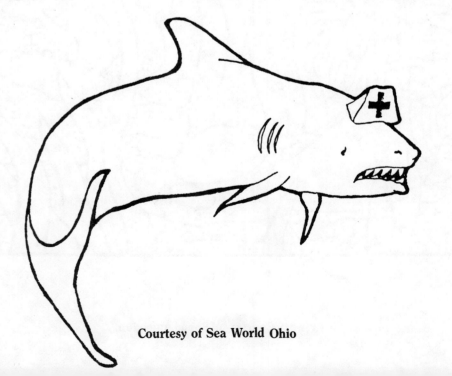

Courtesy of Sea World Ohio

CHAPTER 4

Food Chains...
Come and Eat!

Food Chains: Where does the energy go? Food chains in themselves are usually fairly simple and may include no more than two or three links. Interlocking food chains form food webs. Food webs are a part of every ecosystem because few animals rely on a single source of food, and seldom is any food source consumed by just one kind of animal. The bottom of the food chain is dominated by a great number of very small animals, such as copepods. As the chain grows in length, the size of the animals at each level increases. Link by link, each successive level tends to be made up of larger types of animals.

The flow of energy through such chains is best visualized as a pyramid. The base of the pyramid is formed by vast numbers of microscopic organisms. The top of the pyramid has a few large, predatory animals. From base to top, each succeeding level tends to be dominated by larger organisms which are preying on animals smaller than themselves.

Large size is advantageous in that it is often more difficult to catch and eat a large animal than a small one. However, large animals require large amounts of food to support their size. Special demands are placed on warm blooded animals which live in cold seas, since they must maintain a body temperature well above ambient temperatures. They often must also expend considerable amounts of energy in pursuit of their prey. Such animals devote a great deal of energy to maintaining life. Only a little energy is available for growth and reproduction. These limitations help explain why there are a few large animals at the top of the pyramid depending upon billions of minute organisms at the base.

The transfer of energy from the base to peak of the pyramid is governed by the ''10%'' rule. Simply put, nine-tenths of the food value is lost as heat to the environment at each level of the pyramid. Only about one-tenth of the available energy transfers from one level to the next.

In the following pyramid we see that 10,000 pounds of diatoms are needed to produce 1,000 pounds of zooplankton which produces 100 pounds of fish and squid. The 10 pounds of seal produced by feeding on fish and squid will yield only 1 pound of killer whale. Each pound of whale is supported by 10,000 pounds of phytoplankton. The inefficient transfer of energy limits the number of killer whales which can live and reproduce. It also means killer whales must work hard to obtain the amount of food they need.

Obviously, it is energetically advantageous to feed on organisms close to the base of the pyramid. Baleen whales (the whale at the third level of the pyramid) exemplify this strategy since they feed directly on zooplankton (krill). The 10,000 pounds of diatoms necessary to support 1 pound of killer whale will produce 100 pounds of baleen whale. This helps to explain why blue whales, the largest animals that ever lived, are plankton feeding whales. Baleen whales can afford to be both large and numerous, since they can obtain a large amount of krill with relatively little expenditure of energy.

Courtesy of Seattle Aquarium

Activities in This Chapter

Food Pyramid
From diatoms to killer whales, study this food pyramid to see who eats who.

Maze
Complete this maze to get the snail to its seaweed lunch.

Find-a-Word
Complete the word search and matching activities to review important food chain vocabulary.

Sea Food Chain
Number the pictures to form a sea food chain. The Sun is number one.

Catching Food Crossword Puzzle
Find out all the different ways animals catch their food by completing this crossword puzzle.

Predator-Prey
Draw a line from the hungry animal to its meal.

Food Pyramid

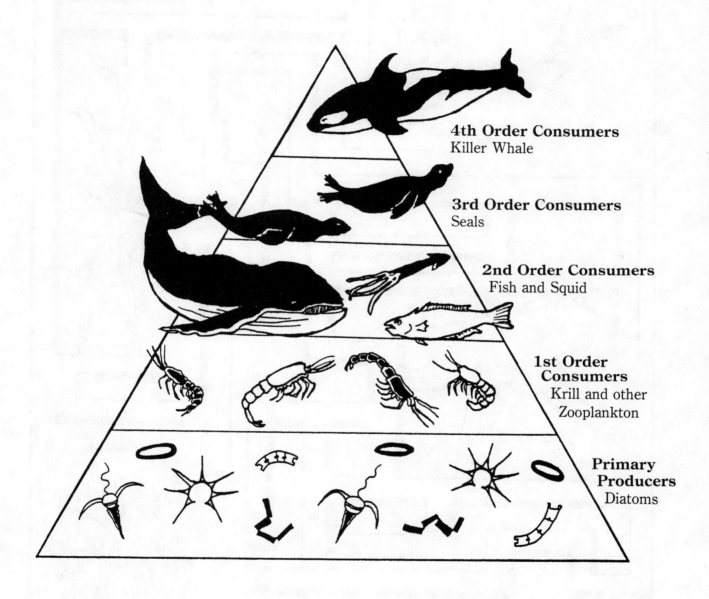

4th Order Consumers
Killer Whale

3rd Order Consumers
Seals

2nd Order Consumers
Fish and Squid

1st Order Consumers
Krill and other Zooplankton

Primary Producers
Diatoms

Courtesy of Seattle Aquarium

Maze

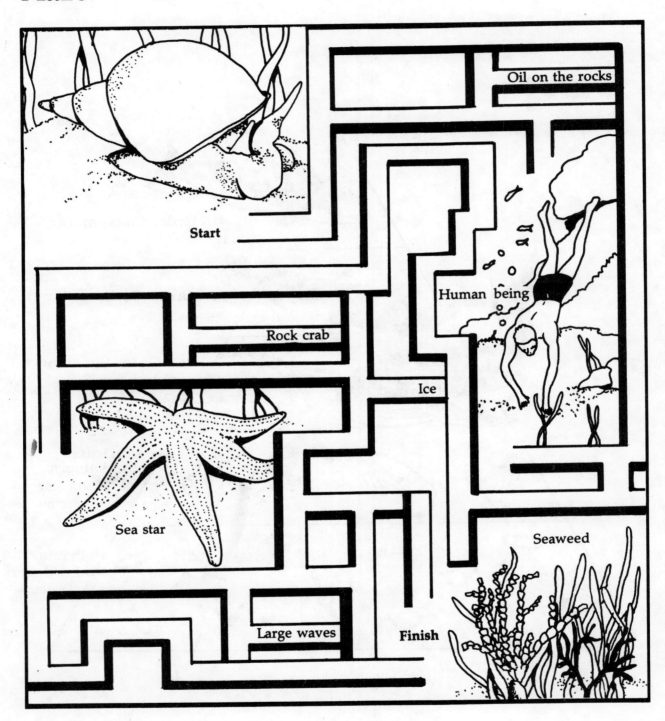

Suppose you are a periwinkle (snail). Can you get through the maze to lunch on some seaweed? Be careful! You could take the wrong turn to danger.

Courtesy of Mystic Aquarium

Find-a-Word

In the puzzle below, look for the vocabulary words listed. Then do the matching exercises.

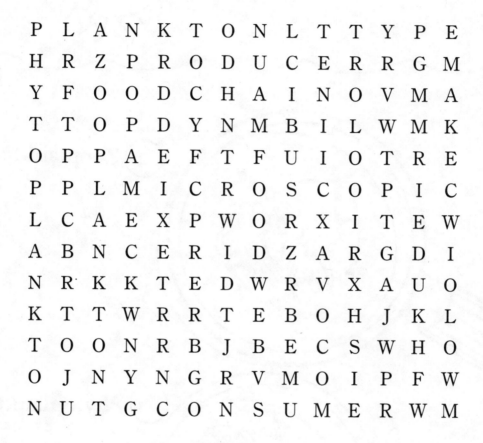

```
P  L  A  N  K  T  O  N  L  T  T  Y  P  E
H  R  Z  P  R  O  D  U  C  E  R  R  G  M
Y  F  O  O  D  C  H  A  I  N  O  V  M  A
T  T  O  P  D  Y  N  M  B  I  L  W  M  K
O  P  P  A  E  F  T  F  U  I  O  T  R  E
P  P  L  M  I  C  R  O  S  C  O  P  I  C
L  C  A  E  X  P  W  O  R  X  I  T  E  W
A  B  N  C  E  R  I  D  Z  A  R  G  D  I
N  R  K  K  T  E  D  W  R  V  X  A  U  O
K  T  T  W  R  R  T  E  B  O  H  J  K  L
T  O  O  N  R  B  J  B  E  C  S  W  H  O
O  J  N  Y  N  G  R  V  M  O  I  P  F  W
N  U  T  G  C  O  N  S  U  M  E  R  W  M
```

Match the definition to the word by putting the letter of the correct definition in the space by the word.

_____ 1. Plankton

_____ 2. Food Web

_____ 3. Phytoplankton

_____ 4. Producer

_____ 5. Consumer

_____ 6. Food Chain

_____ 7. Zooplankton

_____ 8. Microscopic

A. Plant life which, through photosynthesis, traps the Sun's energy and produces food.

B. Drifters and floaters in the sea.

C. A series of plants and animals linked by their feeding relationships.

D. Food chains which overlap and interconnect.

E. Microscopic plants which drift in the sea.

G. Animals which feed on plants or animals.

H. Small animals which drift in the sea.

I. Very small; can be seen only with microscopes.

Sea Food Chain

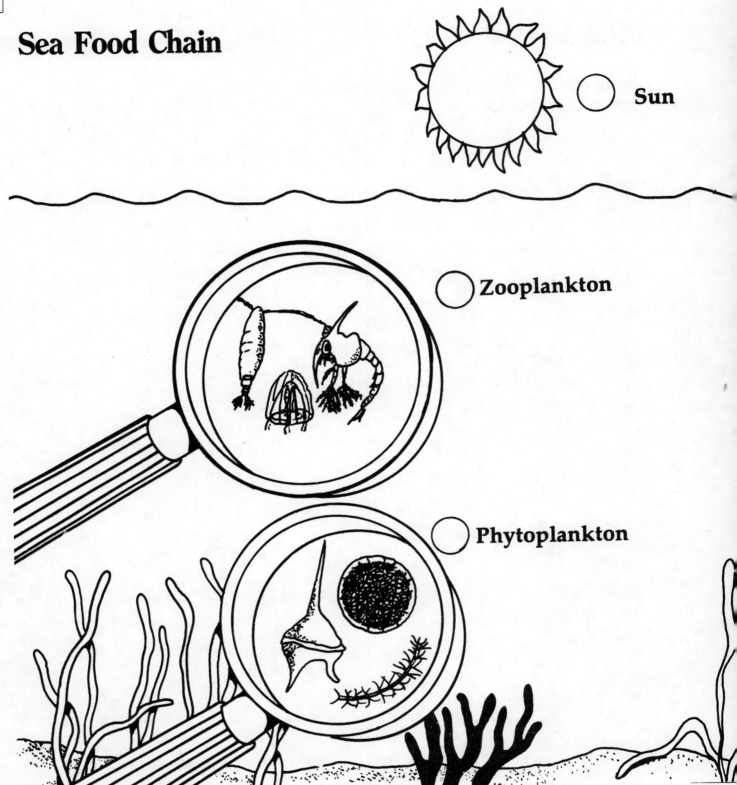

Sun

Zooplankton

Phytoplankton

Sea animals depend upon the sun, plants, and each other to live. Some animals eat plants, some eat other animals, and some eat the decomposed

Courtesy of Mystic Aquarium

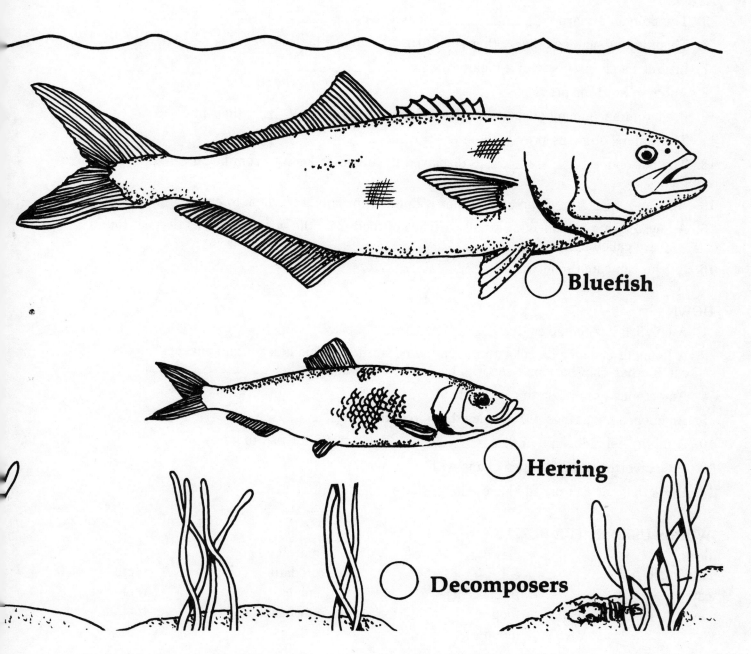

Bluefish

Herring

Decomposers

material of plants and animals. Connect the food chain in the correct order by writing in the circle the number in the order it should appear. Start with the sun and label it number 1.

Catching Food Crossword Puzzle

Marine animals have many adaptations that help them attract, catch and eat food. They have claws and spines, teeth and tentacles, and disguises that help them hide from their prey.

ACROSS

3. The dolphin's sharp _____ help it to catch fish.

6. This kind of snail smothers other shell fish with its one large foot.

7. Lizards catch insects with a flick of their _____.

8. Another word for prey.

9. Predators have many adaptations that help them _____ their prey.

11. This animal stuns its prey with an electric shock.

12. The poisonous _____ displayed by a lionfish keep it from being eaten by other fish.

13. A _____ is an animal that is hunting for another animal to eat.

15. An oyster eats by collecting small particles of food from the water. Animals that eat this way are called _____ _____.

16. A crab can catch food with its _____.

DOWN

1. A jellyfish has tentacles that _____ its prey.

2. A flounder changes its color to match the ocean floor. This hides it and enables it to catch other fish that don't see it. This kind of coloring is called _____.

4. An octopus uses these to catch fish.

5. Anemones have rings of tentacles that circle their _____.

10. A moray eel hides in a dark _____ and waits for fish to go by.

12. This invertebrate prys open clams with its arms.

14. Birds that eat fish usually have a long, sharp _____.

WORDS USED IN THE PUZZLE

beak	claws	mouth	sting
camouflage	eel	predator	teeth
catch	filter feeders	spines	tentacles
cave	food	starfish	tongue
	moon		

Courtesy of National Aquarium in Baltimore

Catching Food Crossword Puzzle

Courtesy of National Aquarium in Baltimore

Predator–Prey

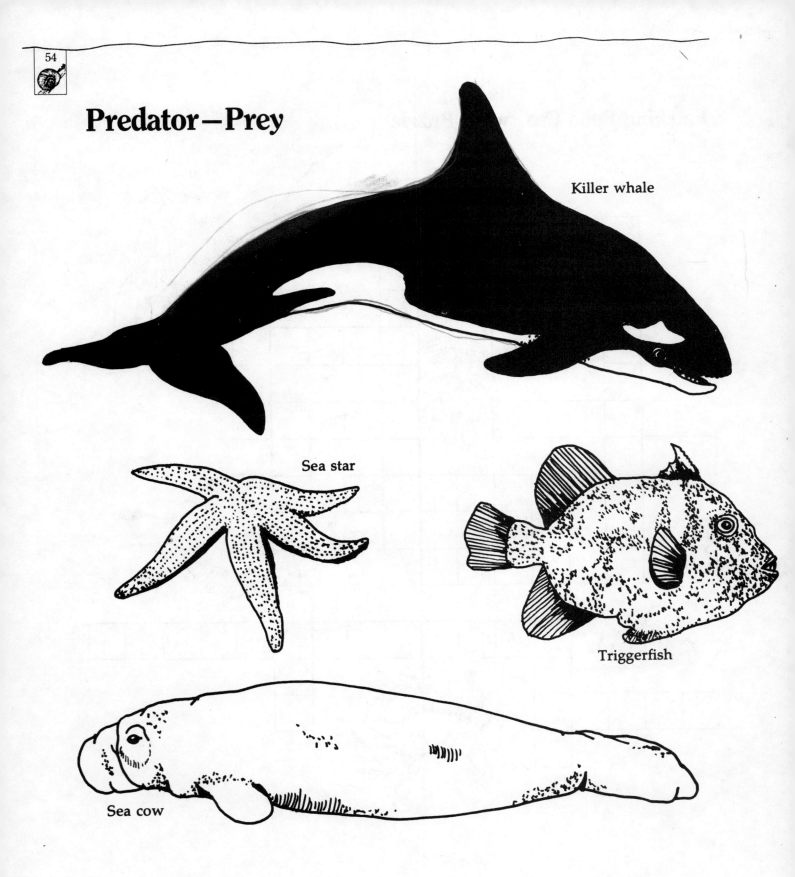

Killer whale

Sea star

Triggerfish

Sea cow

Some animals are predators and some are prey. An animal that hunts another for food is a predator. The animal being hunted is the prey. Flesh eating animals are called carnivores. Animals that eat only plants and grasses are called herbivores.

Courtesy of Mystic Aquarium

Predator—Prey

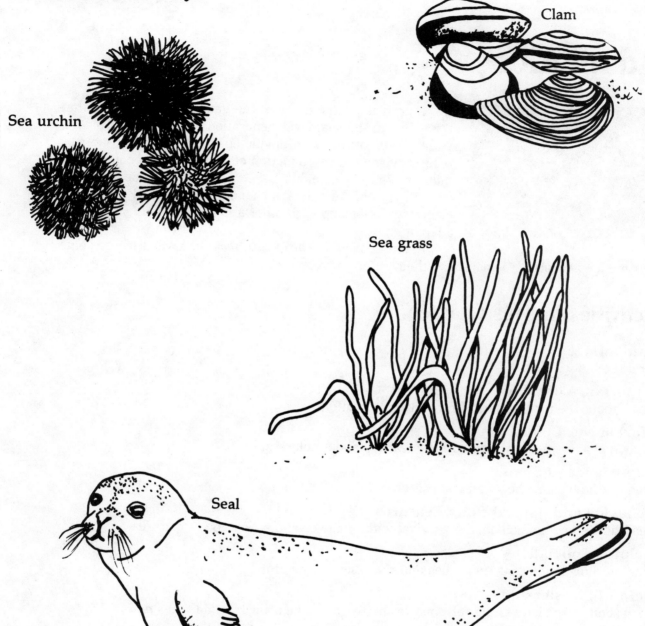

Sea urchin

Clam

Sea grass

Seal

Draw a line from the predator to its prey. One of the animals is not a hunter of other animals, but an herbivore. Which animal is it? Draw a line to the plant it eats.

Courtesy of Mystic Aquarium

CHAPTER 5

Adaptation

Survival . . . the name of the game for the animals that live in the sea. Over generations, nature has provided sea creatures with unique characteristics that increase their survival and reproduction chances. It is no coincidence that certain animals exhibit specific color patterns, or live where they do. An animal's shape, behavior, body parts and even its relationship with other animals are all examples of adaptation.

In this section of *The Ocean Book,* you will discover some ways marine animals have adapted to their water environment.

Activities in This Chapter

Camouflage
Find the hidden fish.

Importance of Color
Read about the many types of protective coloration.

Worksheet: Coloration
A good chance to see what you have learned about coloration.

Importance of Shape
Find out how shape helps animals survive.

Behavior and Special Body Features
Read how some animals insure survival with behavior and special body features.

Helpful Appendages
Find out how spines, suction tubes and tentacles are helpful.

Helpful Partnerships
Read about some interesting relationships between marine animals, and learn a new word, too.

Adaptation Code
By cracking this code you will learn more adaptation vocabulary.

The Six Senses of Fish
Learn about the unique ways fish see, feel, hear, touch, and navigate.

Identifying Hawaiian Fish
Some of the most beautiful fish in the world live among the coral reefs of the Pacific. Unscramble and color these ten Hawaiian fishes.

Schooling Fishsticks
Demonstrate how fish school and travel together.

Camouflage

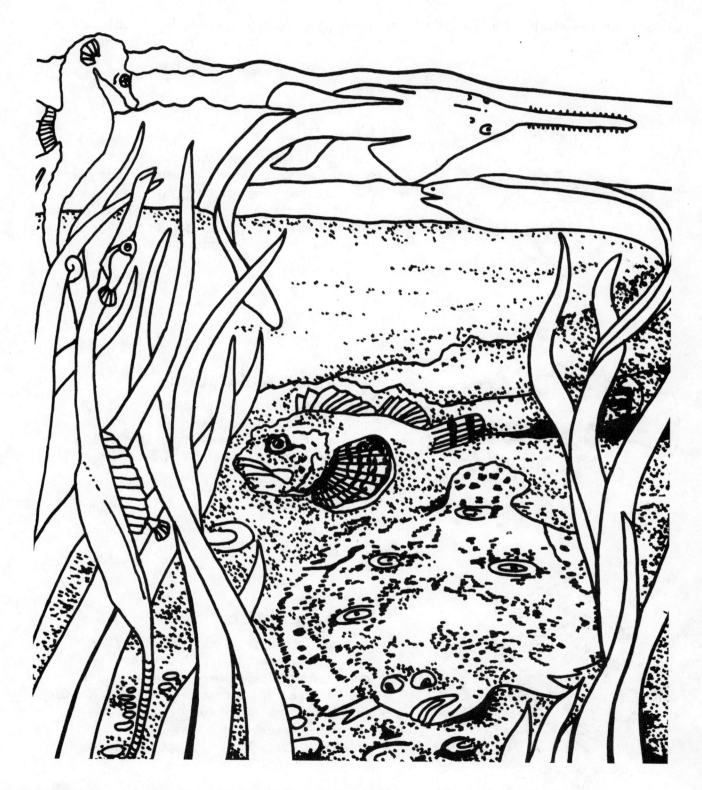

Find and color the fishes hidden in this drawing.

Importance of Color

Coloration may help hide an animal or draw attention to its role in an animal community.

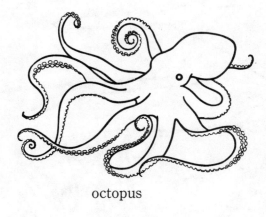

octopus

Camouflage

Camouflage coloration helps animals blend in with their surroundings. The octopus changes color instantly from black to gray to red to match its background. It can also change the texture of its skin, becoming bumpy or smooth to blend in with rocks and seaweeds.

clown triggerfish

Disruptive Coloration

Spots and stripes break up the body shape of some fishes and conceal them against their backgrounds. This kind of camouflage, called disruptive coloration, is common in coral reef fishes.

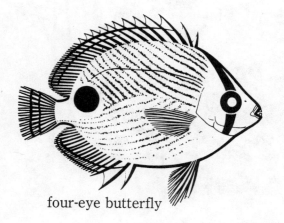

four-eye butterfly

False Eye Spots

Unusual color patterns may hide vulnerable parts of an animal's body. The true eyes of a four-eye butterflyfish are hidden in a band of black, but near the tail are two prominent "false eyes." A confused predator may attack these instead of the real eyes, allowing the butterflyfish to escape in the opposite direction.

Countershading

penguin

Many open ocean animals have dark backs and light bellies. This protective coloration is called countershading. Viewed from above, dark backs blend with the darkness of the deep ocean. From below, it is difficult for predators to see light bellies against bright sunlit surface waters.

Advertising Coloration

cleaner wrasse

Some animals have coloration that attracts attention and advertises a special service. Cleaner fishes help other fishes by removing harmful parasites from their skin. Predators recognize the bright color patterns of cleaners and do not harm them because of the useful service they perform.

Warning

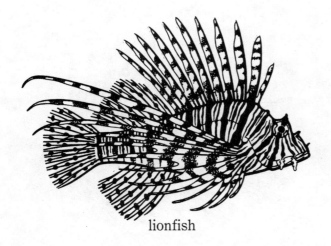

lionfish

Some animals are so well protected with spines, poisons, and armor that their coloration is a warning for other species to stay away. The lionfish has brightly striped fins with poisonous spines that it displays to would-be attackers.

Worksheet: Coloration

1. **Protective Coloration** helps animals survive in their natural habitats. Protect the fish below by giving them the proper coloration:

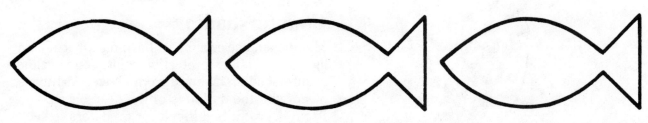

Countershading   **Disruptive Coloration**   **False Eye Spots**

2. What is **Advertising Coloration** and how does it help an animal survive?

_____

_____

_____

_____

cleaner wrasse

3. What is **Camouflage** and how does it help an animal survive?

_____

_____

_____

_____

octopus

4. What is **Warning Coloration** and how does it help an animal survive?

_____

_____

_____

_____

lionfish

Courtesy of New England Aquarium

Importance of Shape

Body shapes give important clues about where fishes live and how they move.

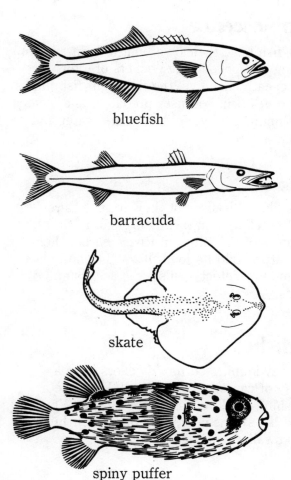

bluefish

barracuda

skate

spiny puffer

wolffish

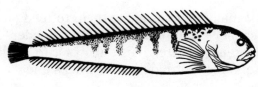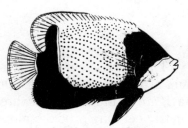

majestic angelfish

Fusiform: the swiftest of all fishes

Powerful tails help them chase prey and avoid predators. Many of them live in the open ocean and swim continuously, traveling thousands of miles in their lifetimes.

Rod: elongated, arrow-like fishes

These hunters ambush their prey. They float motionless until a smaller fish swims near. Then they lunge out with lightning speed to seize their victim.

Depressed: flat, pancake-shaped fishes

They use camouflage instead of speed for survival. To escape predators they burrow into the sand or mud. Many change the color of their skin to match their surroundings.

Sphere: puffers and balloonfishes

When threatened they fill their bodies with water or air, becoming too big to swallow. Some have spines all over their bodies for added protection.

Ribbon: snake-like fishes

They are slow swimmers but move easily through cracks and crevices, under rocks and around aquatic plants. They are secretive, hiding from predators and ambushing prey that come too near their hiding places.

Compressed: fishes flattened from side to side

When viewed head-on these thin fishes almost seem to disappear. They are common on coral reefs. Their compressed bodies allow them to make quick sharp turns and dart in and out of hiding places.

Courtesy of New England Aquarium

Behavior and Special Body Features

Many animals combine behavior and special body features to insure their survival.

flashlight fish

Bioluminescence

Flashlight fish have their own built-in light system. By covering and uncovering pockets of glowing bacteria beneath each eye, the flashlight fish blinks signals to other fish, confuses predators and locates food. Flashlight fish live in deep, dark water and hunt only at night.

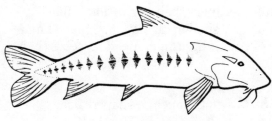

Amazon catfish

Barbels

They look like whiskers but they are not hairs. Barbels are feeling- and tasting-organs. In the murky waters of the Amazon River, barbels help the giant catfish find its food. It touches and tastes the river mud to detect snails, crustaceans and other foods.

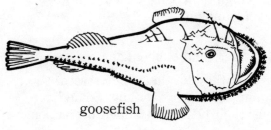

goosefish

Anglerfishes

Some slow-swimming bottom dwellers have a special way of capturing their food. They use a fleshy "fishing lure" to attract their prey. When an interested fish swims near, they open their huge mouths to swallow the victim.

long-nose butterflyfish

Strange Mouths

The mouths of many animals allow them to feed on foods others cannot catch or eat. The long slender snout of the long-nose butterflyfish allows it to feed on tiny invertebrates that hide in the cracks and crevices of the coral reef.

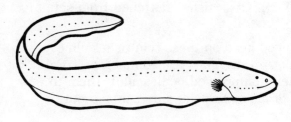

electric eel

Electricity

Several fishes have special body organs that produce electricity. The electric eel sets up a low voltage electric field around its body that helps it detect food and navigate in muddy river waters. If threatened, the electric eel may produce more powerful discharges, up to 800 volts.

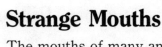

Courtesy of New England Aquarium

Helpful Appendages

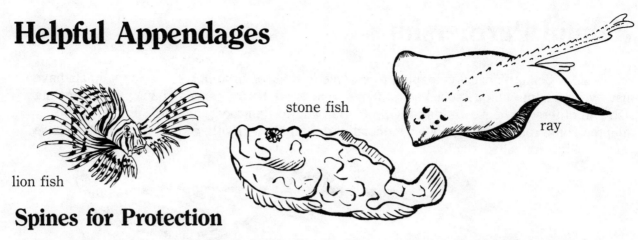

lion fish

stone fish

ray

Spines for Protection

Many fish which are not fast swimmers have sharp or poisonous spines for protection. The lion fish, scorpion fish and stone fish have venomous dorsal spines along their backs. Stingrays have a poisonous dart on their tail.

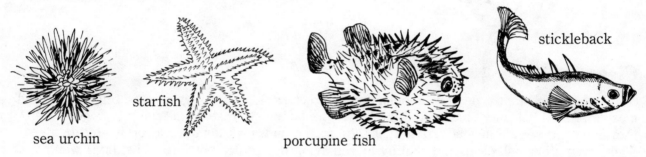

sea urchin

starfish

porcupine fish

stickleback

Some sea urchins and starfish have their upper surfaces protected by sharp spines. The stickleback and triggerfish have dorsal spines they can erect and lock in place to keep from being swallowed. The porcupine fish is also covered with spines which it erects by inflating itself like a balloon.

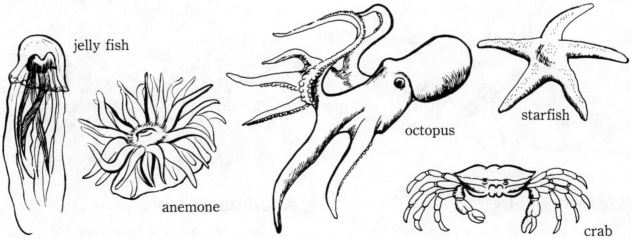

jelly fish

anemone

octopus

starfish

crab

Arms and Tentacles for Catching and Holding

Some sea animals, like starfish and octopus, have arms equipped with suction tubes or discs for catching and tenaciously holding their food. Some lobsters, crabs and shrimp have pinching claws on the ends of their appendages. Jelly fish and sea anemones have tentacles equipped with stinging cells to catch their food.

Helpful Partnerships

Besides being physically adapted to survive in their environments, marine animals have also evolved some unique social adaptations to improve their chances of survival. Schooling fish join others of their own kind for protection and to find food; but some animals have adapted some rather strange but beneficial partnerships with other kinds of animals. These relationships are called symbiosis.

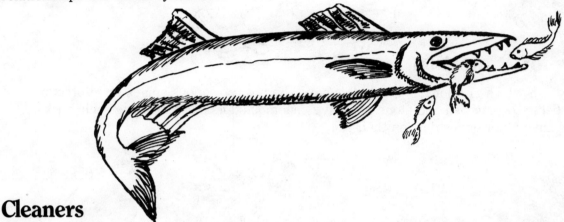

Cleaners

A very important type of relationship in the reef world exists between the brightly colored cleaner fish and cleaner shrimp and the larger predator fish. Instead of trying to conceal themselves, these animals advertise that they are around, for they have a service to offer. They keep other fish clean and healthy by removing bits of dead or infected skin as well as skin parasites and fungus. In return they obtain food and immunity from being eaten.

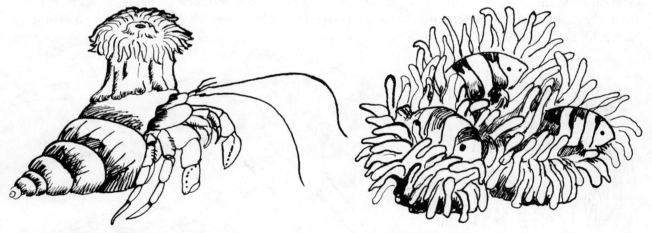

Hermit Crabs

The hermit crab does not have a hard shell of his own but borrows the empty, discarded shells of others. Sea anemones sometimes grow on these shells providing camouflage for the crab's home, and in turn are carried about by the crab to new feeding areas.

Anemone Fish

The brightly colored anemone fish enjoy a safe home for themselves and their young amongst the stinging tentacles of the sea anemone, to which they are immune. In return, their bright colors help lure other fish for the anemone to eat.

Adaptation Code

A. _ _ _ _ _ _ _ _ _ _
   3 1 13 15 21 6 12 1 7 5

An animal blends with its background to hide from its enemies.

B. _ _ _ _ _ _ _ _ _
   19 25 13 2 9 15 19 9 19

Two kinds of animals living together to survive.

C. _ _ _ _ _ _ _ _ _
   20 5 18 18 9 20 15 18 25

A certain place an animal lives and defends.

D. _ _ _ _ _ _ _ _ _
   19 3 8 15 15 12 9 14 7

Many of the same fish swimming together.

E. _ _ _ _ _ _ _ _ _
   18 8 5 15 20 1 24 9 19

Fishes swimming into a current.

F. _ _ _ _ _ _ _ _ _ _
   1 20 20 1 3 8 13 5 14 20

The way in which sea star tube feet hold on to a surface.

Alphabet	A	B	C	D	E	F	G	H	I	J	K	L	M	N	O	P	Q	R	S	T	U	V	W	X	Y	Z
Code	1	2	3	4	5	6	7	8	9	10	11	12	13	14	15	16	17	18	19	20	21	22	23	24	25	26

Look at the alphabet code. Place the correct letter in the space above its matching number to decode the adaptation word that is opposite its meaning.

The Six Senses of Fish

Aquatic animals have senses adapted for seeing, hearing, feeling, tasting and smelling in the water. Fishes have a sixth sense, the remarkable lateral line.

Seeing

Fish have no necks so they cannot turn their heads. Their large round eyes protrude from the sides of their heads giving them a wider field of vision. Have you ever seen a picture taken with a wide angle "fish eye" camera lens? If so, you know how much more can be seen at one time than with a common flat camera lens (which is much like your eye). The no neck problem has been solved by crustaceans (lobster, crabs and shrimp) by having their eyes on moveable stalks.

Hearing

People have called the oceans the "silent sea," because our ears are not adapted to hearing very well in the water. The sea is anything but silent. Sound travels very well in water (almost 5 times faster than in air) and marine animals have many ways of making sounds. Most marine animals have highly sensitive hearing. We have had to construct hydrophones and sonar receivers to hear as well. Some fish, like the electric eel, use electrical impulses (much like sonar) to locate their food.

Feeling, Touching and Tasting

Fish have a unique device called a lateral line. This is a row of sensory nerves along each side of their bodies which are sensitive to movement and pressure changes in the water around them. Sightless fish that live in dark underground caves depend on these lateral lines to find food and to navigate.

Many bottom dwellers which have hard shells, protective spines or tentacles have no need for eyes, but use their sense of touch to find food. The tentacles of anemones and the tube feet of starfish and sea urchins are used to sense food.

The catfish which feeds on the bottom has eyes to watch for predators, but feels for his food with his whisker-like chin barbs that are sensitive to touch, and are also covered with taste buds.

Smelling

Many predators, like sharks and eels, use their sense of smell to locate food. Salmon are thought to be able to find their way across hundreds of miles of open ocean to their home streams by means of this sense.

Identifying Hawaiian Fish!

Before unscrambling the letters, try to identify the fish by how they look. Which fish has a mask and looks like a bandit?

ANGEL FISH
BANDIT FISH
BUTTERFLY FISH
DAMSEL FISH
GOAT FISH

LION FISH
PARROT FISH
SQUIRREL FISH
STICK FISH
SURGEON FISH

1 DITNAB
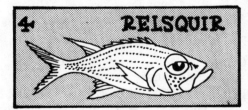

6 NEOGURS

2 TAGO
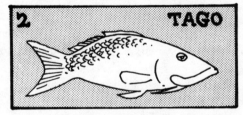

7 INOL

3 KICTS
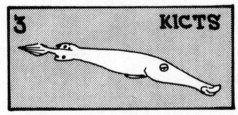

8 TUBERFLYT

4 RELSQUIR

9 SAMELD

5 TARROP

10 ELGNA

Courtesy of Sea Life Park, Hawaii

Schooling Fishsticks (For the Teacher)

Objective
By acting as a school of lanternfish, students learn how bioluminescence and schooling behavior help fish survive.

Background for Teachers
Each species of deep sea lanternfish shines with a unique pattern of body lights. Without its lights a black lanternfish would be hard to see in the darkness of the deep sea. The bioluminescent spots help fish find mates and lure prey. The lights help lanternfish form schools to avoid or confuse predators. (You can discuss such lanternfish adaptations with students throughout the activity, asking questions like those in italics below.)

Materials
One 24-inch stick or dowel per student; Copies of lanternfish pattern (both sides); Cardboard for mounting fish patterns; Black indelible marker, scotch tape, glue.

Getting Started
Group the paper fish into schools (four or five per school). To give each school a unique pattern of lights, use the marker to darken specific spots on each fish in that school. (The light patterns on both sides of a fish should match. Each school has a different pattern, but fish in the same school have the same pattern.) Attach the fish to sticks.

Forming Schools
Mix up the fishsticks. Give a fishstick to each student. *Ask students to guess where lanternfish live. Why are they called lanternfish? Explain that each species of lanternfish has a unique pattern of body lights.* Each student holds a fishstick high and looks for other fish with the same light pattern. Lookalikes unite to form a school. Have each school of student-fish list ideas about how bioluminescence helps lanternfish survive.

Schooling for Survival
Let each school of student-fish swim a simple course, following these rules:

- The fish swim close together, but without touching.
- All fish in a school maintain the same speed and direction.
- The front fish of the school determines the direction and speed for all.
- Each time the school turns, the front fish becomes the new leader.
- A school that is forced to divide must reunite as soon as possible.

How did students feel about being part of a school? Was it easy to move as a group? What cues did they use to stay together? Would it be harder to school in the dark? How does schooling help fish?
To show how fish school to survive, you can have many species unite to form a huge school, using the same rules. Have the school swim a fixed course while you play the predator. Attack the school, but only capture those fish who leave the ranks. The school may change direction to avoid you, but it must stick to the course. (No running.) If a fish turns or changes speed to avoid a predator, the rest of the school must follow. A fish who's caught becomes a predator and may help attack the school. The game ends when the school reaches the end of the course. *Was it different being in a large school? Is it better to be at the outer edge or in the middle of the school? If predators joined in a school, would they feed more effectively?*

Follow-Up
Visit an aquarium to observe fish schools. *Do real fish follow the same rules for schooling? What land animals work together in groups? How are they different from schools of fish?*

Getting Ready

Make a copy of this lanternfish pattern (both sides) for each student. For BIG impact, enlarge the fish to double size on an enlarging copy machine. Cut out the pattern. Mount a fish half on either side of cardboard to form a sturdy lanternfish.

Courtesy of Monterey Bay Aquarium

Ecosystems

An ecosystem consists of all the living organisms and the non-living things within a specific area. For example, a sandy beach ecosystem consists of all the animals and plants plus the physical features like sand, sun and sea. There are many different types of marine ecosystems, such as marshes, sandy beaches, rocky beaches, estuaries, kelp forests and coral reefs. To understand the marine environment, it is important to know about more than just the animals which live in an area. The physical conditions affecting the environment are important as are the biological and behavioral interrelationships among different animals. Both the physical and biological environments affect an organism's ability to survive.

The several different types of ecosystems presented in this section of *The Ocean Book* provide a look at the important interrelationships within various ecosystems.

Activities in This Chapter

Tidepools and Tidepool Word Search
Find out about the plants and animals that live in tidepools.

Estuary 3-D Board
Estuaries form where fresh water mixes with salt water. This art project will teach more about this special environment.

Beach Walk Word Search
How many of these animals can you find?

Coral Reef
Study the animals that live among the coral reefs. Color this picture for fun.

Design a Beach
Use the list of plants and animals provided to design either a rocky or sandy beach. Study the list, and find picture examples before you begin.

Protect This Natural Habitat
Cut out and paste the pictures about fur seals at their rocky rookery.

Sea Side Riddles
Are you a SEA STAR? Answer the riddles and find out.

At the Beach
Explore the beach using your own beach log and the techniques described.

Tidepools

What is a tidepool?

Along the rocky shores of New England the tide rises and falls twice each day, creating a strip of land known as the intertidal zone. This zone is covered by water during high tide and exposed to the air when the tide is low. As the tide recedes, pools of water, called tidepools, are left behind in the cracks and crevices of the rocky shore.

What lives in a tidepool?

Most of the animals found in a tidepool are invertebrates—animals without backbones. These animals include sea stars, sea urchins, crabs, sea anemones, periwinkles, and mussels. Tidepools are also filled with a variety of seaweeds such as sea lettuce, rockweed, and Irish moss. The plants and animals that live in tidepools are well adapted to the harsh conditions of this environment. They must be able to withstand the drying effects of low tide, crashing waves, and rapid changes in temperature and salinity.

Animals and plants live in different areas of the rocky shore according to their needs. Animals that must always be wet, like sea anemones and sea urchins, live below the low tide mark. Others, like the periwinkles and mussels, hold water in their shells and can live in areas uncovered at low tide. Crabs and sea stars move to follow the tide or hide among seaweeds and under rocks to stay wet.

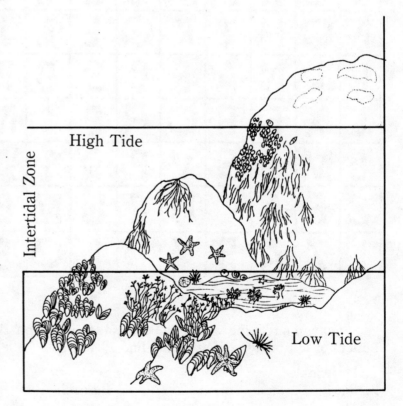

Tidepool Word Search

P	T	H	E	R	M	I	T	C	R	A	B	A	R
E	I	R	O	C	K	W	E	E	D	Q	L	N	M
R	D	O	S	E	A	U	R	C	H	I	N	E	U
I	E	F	E	L	S	C	A	L	L	O	P	M	S
W	P	B	A	R	N	A	C	L	E	V	U	O	S
I	O	W	S	M	U	Z	R	G	F	A	H	N	E
N	O	H	T	K	Q	L	A	J	I	B	S	E	L
K	L	N	A	P	B	S	B	P	S	O	P	K	S
L	X	E	R	O	H	F	L	N	H	K	O	J	L
E	M	I	S	V	R	D	T	W	X	E	N	I	M
S	E	A	C	U	C	U	M	B	E	R	G	B	D
L	Z	A	R	Y	D	L	O	B	S	T	E	R	A

Find and circle the words that are hidden in the puzzle. All the words read from top to bottom or left to right. You should find 15 words.

1. Periwinkle
2. Fish
3. Mussel
4. Scallop
5. Sea urchin

6. Sea star
7. Barnacle
8. Sea cucumber
9. Rockweed
10. Anemone

11. Sponge
12. Lobster
13. Crab
14. Tidepool
15. Hermit crab

Estuary 3-D Board

A healthy estuary fringed by its streams, marshes, and shores forms a very productive biological system. The marshes provide nutrients to the estuary which cycles efficiently from plants to animals to soil and around again through the food web. The marshes provide undisturbed nursery grounds, and the life cycles of the plants and animals maintain a natural balance.

When man enters the estuary environment, he makes changes. He catches fish, dredges oysters, digs for clams and traps crabs. In addition, he adds undesirable substances to the water: industrial chemical wastes; large quantities of nutrients from municipal sewage discharges; and the silt and sediment runoff from construction sites. To keep navigable channels clear, to provide sites for dredging spoils and create more land for construction, marshes are often drained and filled. Tankers pump their ballast tanks and cause oil slicks. All of these activities disrupt food chains.

An evaluation of the health of an estuary, both idealized and showing man's negative influences, can be accomplished by creating a 3-dimensional board which when looked at from one side indicates the conditions that make a healthy estuary, and when turned around shows how man interferes, inadvertently or intentionally, with the estuarine system.

Get these supplies:

Corregated Cardboard

cut slits for the tabs

Thin cardboard—cut into squares, with tabs on the bottom

don't forget clean-up materials.

paints, crayons, scissors, markers, knife, water for paints.

Courtesy of Smithsonian Environmental Research Center

Make An Estuary Environmental Board

MATERIALS
corrugated cardboard at least 25 cm
   by 25 cm for base (one per
   person)
thin cardboard pieces usable on
   both sides (10 per person)
magic markers
paint
knife (to make slits in base)
crayons
scissors

Preparation

Cut some of the thin cardboard into squares (see illustration) with tabs on the bottom. Cut slits for tabs in one piece of the base (corrugated cardboard) to use as a demonstration. For younger groups you may want to make slits in bases ahead of time.

Procedure

1. Explain to the participants that they are display designers of a museum with the task of making a 3-dimensional model of an estuary. They have already completed the background research. The model is to be viewed from two sides. When it is looked at one way, the model is to show a healthy estuary ecosystem, and when turned around, it is to show how man can upset the balance of the system.

2. Demonstrate how to make the board using the base with slits and one of the pre-cut thin cardboard pieces. Draw a member of a food chain, such as a fish, on one side and a man-made disturbance, such as a man fishing, on the other. Put the tabs of the piece into the slits on the base. Turn the board so participants can view both sides.

Courtesy of Smithsonian Environmental Research Center

3. Give each person a baseboard and some thin cardboard pieces to design an estuary board. When all the cardboard pieces are in place, the baseboard can be decorated. It may be necessary for the leader to cut the slits in the baseboard.

4. Discuss the participants' boards; have them explain the subjects chosen.

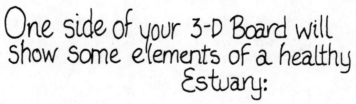

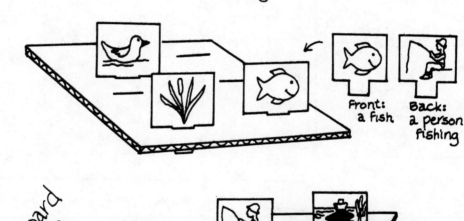

Questions

1. Are all of man's interferences in the estuary harmful?

2. Do natural forces, such as hurricanes, also upset the equilibrium in an estuary? How?

3. How would an addition of fertilizer affect an estuary? Kepone? Herbicides?

Other Ideas:

An alternate board could be constructed to demonstrate what participants like about the estuary, such as swimming or sailing, and what they dislike, such as stinging nettles.

Courtesy of Smithsonian Environmental Research Center

Beach Walk

All of these animals can be found along the beach. Can you find them in the hidden word puzzle? The words may appear horizontally, diagonally, and vertically.

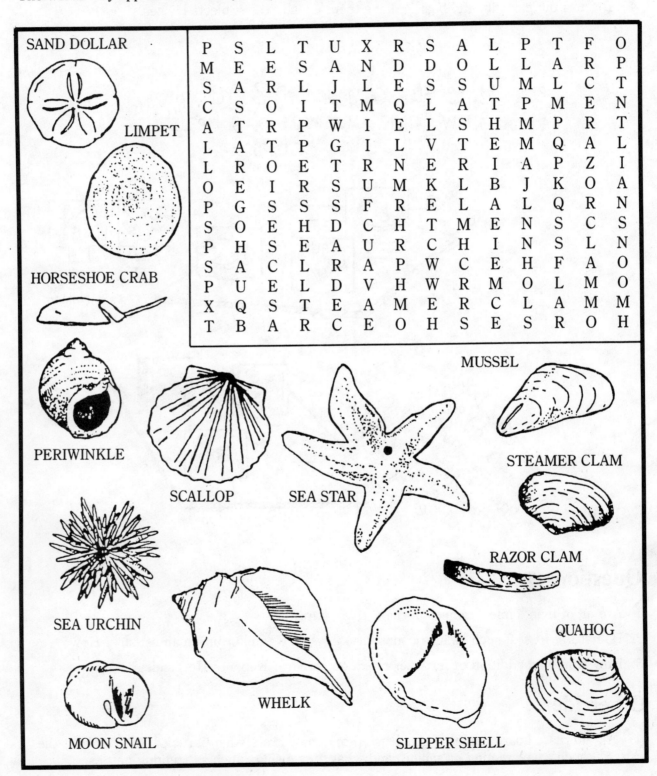

SAND DOLLAR

LIMPET

HORSESHOE CRAB

PERIWINKLE

SCALLOP

SEA STAR

MUSSEL

STEAMER CLAM

SEA URCHIN

WHELK

RAZOR CLAM

SLIPPER SHELL

QUAHOG

MOON SNAIL

```
P S L T U X R S A L P T F O
M E E S A N D D O L L A R P
S A R L J L E S O U M L C T
C S O I T M Q L S H M M R N
A T R P W I E L A E M P E T
L A O P G R L V T M Q R A L
L R I E T U N E R I A P Z I
O E S R S F M K L B J K O A
P G S S D C R L A L Q S R N
S O E H H C H T M E N S C S
P H C A U R P C H I H S L N
S A L L R A C W C E O F A O
P U E L D H W C R M L A M O
X Q S T E A M E H R C L M H
T B A R C E O H S E R A O H
```

Courtesy of Mystic Aquarium

Coral Reef

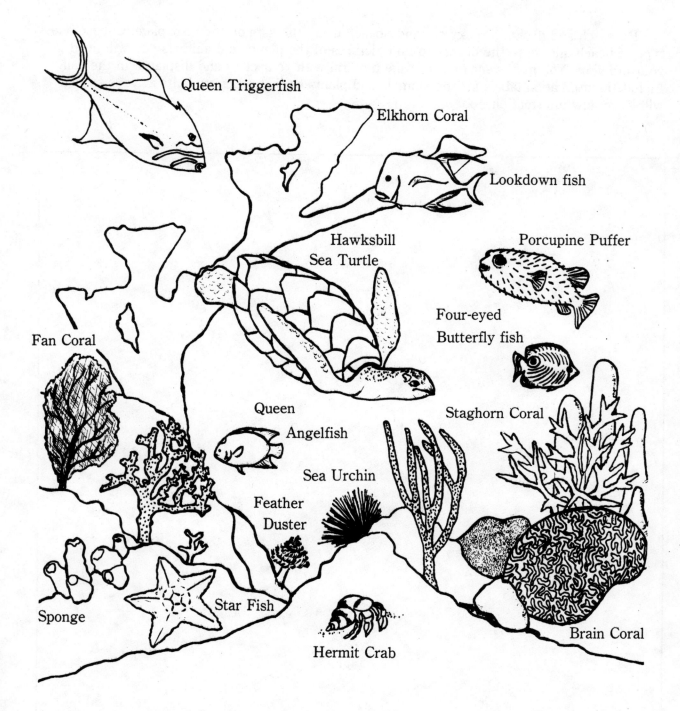

Queen Triggerfish

Elkhorn Coral

Lookdown fish

Hawksbill
Sea Turtle

Porcupine Puffer

Four-eyed
Butterfly fish

Fan Coral

Queen
Angelfish

Staghorn Coral

Sea Urchin

Feather
Duster

Star Fish

Sponge

Hermit Crab

Brain Coral

The colorful coral reef looks like a beautiful underwater garden. It provides a good home for many kinds of animals.

Color This Coral Reef

Design a Beach

Research and design a rocky or sandy beach using the lists on the next page. Choose one type of beach and go to the library to find pictures of the plants and animals you will need in your drawing. You may want to also make a mural with your class and display it in the hall. Include identification labels for the animals and plants so that other students at your school will learn new information, too.

Rocky Beach Habitat

1. brittle sea star
2. barnacles
3. hermit crab
4. sea lettuce
5. mussels
6. sea anemone
7. octupus
8. rockfish
9. harbor seal
10. bald eagle
11. sea cucumber
12. sea urchin

Sandy Beach Habitat

1. cockle
2. little neck clam
3. dungeness crab
4. sunflower sea star
5. sand dollar
6. sand pipers
7. cormorant
8. sea gull
9. jellyfish
10. horseshoe crabs
11. hermit crabs
12. sea oats

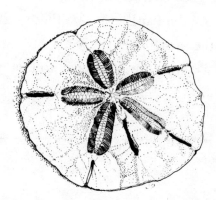

Protect This Natural Habitat

1. Label the water **Bering Sea**.

2. Color the water **blue**.

3. Title the picture, "A June Day At A Rookery."

4. Cut out the **rocky coast**. Glue it in the right hand corner.

5. Cut out the **fur seals**. Glue the **pups** near the **female** on the shore.

6. Cut out the **fish**. Glue them in the sea.

7. Add 3 sea birds by drawing a " 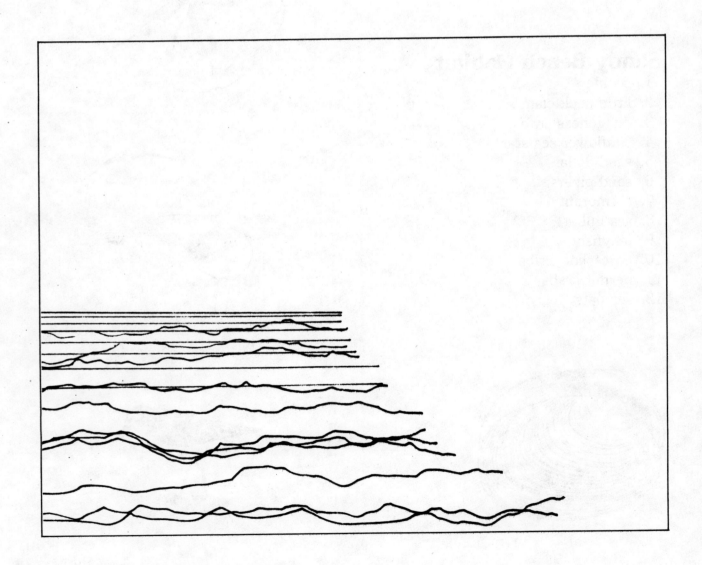 " in the sky.

8. Cut out the **lupines**. Glue these **wild flowers** on the beach away from the fur seals.

9. Let the **sun** shine! Draw a sun.

10. Discuss what would happen to this rookery if some of the living things were destroyed.

Cut-outs for the Habitat Activity

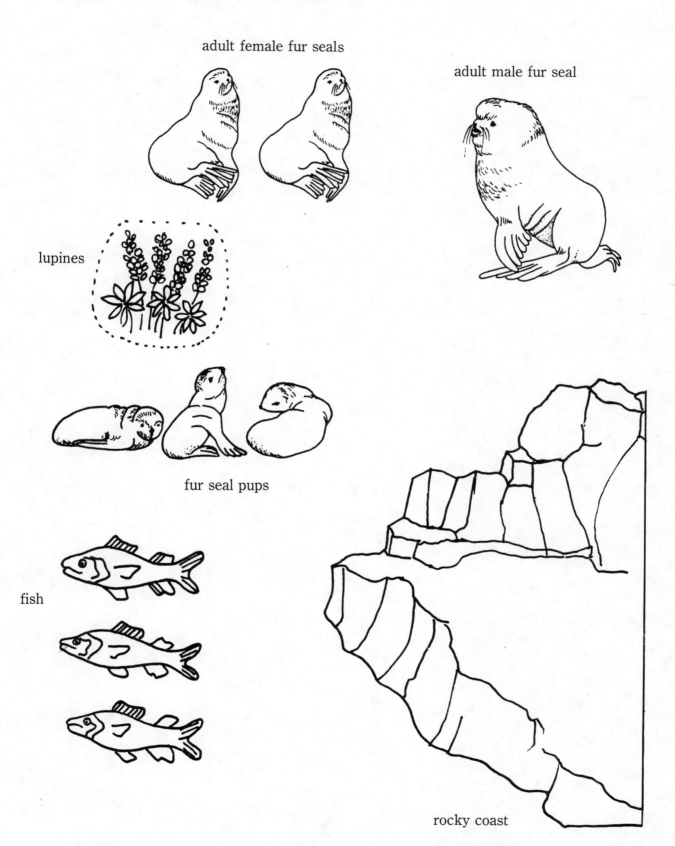

adult female fur seals

adult male fur seal

lupines

fur seal pups

fish

rocky coast

Blank for Cut-out Page

Sea Side Riddles

The riddles below refer to plants and animals found on both coasts of the United States. If you solve the riddle on the first hint you get 20 points. On the second hint you get 15 points, etc. Total your score at the end. If you score over 100 points you are a SEA STAR!

A Little Help

Pelican
Sea Turtle
Barnacle
Hermit crab
Starfish
Kelp
Fiddler crab
Horseshoe crab

1. __ __ __ __ __ __ __ __ __ __ __ __ __

Five pairs of legs this critter has for
Helping it to walk the sea shore.
Domed and slow, it could use many more. _____ 20 pts.

Its tail is sharp, but will not stab.
Its claws are small and will not grab. _____ 15 pts.

On its back it's quite a sight
Cause its legs don't help
Its tail turn it right. _____ 10 pts.

This green-brown animal's blood is blue!
And it's named for a horse's shoe. _____ 5 pts.

2. __ __ __ __ __ __ __ __ __ __ __ __

At the water's edge where they can't be blown,
Sometimes shells walk on their own! _____ 20 pts.

But if you watch them carefully,
Two eyes and many legs you'll see. _____ 15 pts.

These are animals that dwell
Inside another creature's shell. _____ 10 pts.

And when this shell gets too tight
They find another that's just right. _____ 5 pts.

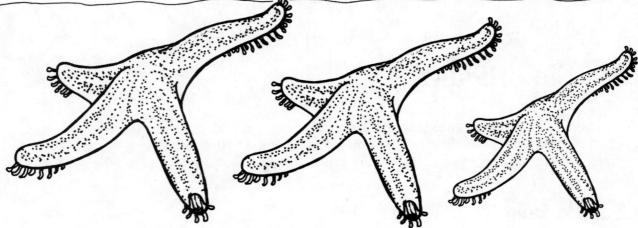

3. __ __ __ __   __ __ __ __   __ __ __ __

In muddy sand banks these abound.
Digging holes into the ground.

At low tide you'll see them all,
With one claw large and one claw small.   _____ 20 pts.

To dig their holes I'm sure they yearn,
To carry sand out in an urn.
But since they can not use such kegs
They take it out stuck to their legs!   _____ 15 pts.

At low tide in groups they eat.
When high tide comes they soon retreat.   _____ 10 pts.

About an inch across the middle
Their big claw looks just like a fiddle.   _____ 5 pts.

4. __ __ __ __ __ __ __ __

This animal makes its house on purpose
For protecting it above the surface.   _____ 20 pts.

This creature encrusts the boats that sail
And also plagues the great grey whale.   _____ 15 pts.

On logs and docks and rocks and piers
To anything hard their shell adheres.   _____ 10 pts.

5. __ __ __ __

This plant can be found on both the coasts
But the biggest type the West Coast boasts.

It grows well over one hundred feet
And sea otters use it for a seat.   _____ 20 pts.

All types of fish do live among
This ocean forest which is strung
From rocky bottom to the sun.   _____ 15 pts.

And even people harvest this
To eat it for a tasty dish.   _____ 10 pts.

If you still need some help,
This plant is the mighty __ __ __ __.   _____ 5 pts.

6. __ __ __ __ __ __ __ __ __

Slowly up the beach they crawl
to dig their bell-shaped nests.
Some fishermen drown them when they trawl
and say that they are pests.

__ 20 pts.

Once many grew to a great size
But now their shell the tourist buys,
To use on glasses for their eyes,
And this had led to their demise.

__ 15 pts.

Although they mainly live at sea
Into their lungs it's air they breathe
And though on land they move quite slow
In the sea they're quick, you know.

__ 10 pts.

Many research teams have tried
To keep these animals alive
But we still aren't sure if they'll survive.

__ 5 pts.

7. __ __ __ __ __ __ __ __

Brown and purple, orange and red,
It seems as if they have no head
But in the center, underneath
there's a small hole with their teeth.

__ 20 pts.

If you wonder how they eat
Believe me, it is quite a feat.
They slowly wrap around a clam
And pull it open when they can.

__ 15 pts.

Five arms *or* legs are the best clue.
A broken one they'll grow anew.

__ 10 pts.

On rocks and beaches and a sand bar
Find them. Just look for a star.

__ 5 pts.

8. __ __ __ __ __ __ __

You'll see these birds along the coast.
Often sitting on a post.
And if you get to see them dive,
You'll be amazed they're still alive.

__ 20 pts.

Across the waves they fly and seek
Fish, which they catch in their beak.

__ 15 pts.

And when they find fish—like a rocket
They catch and hold them in a pocket.
The pocket is part of their bill,
And from it they will eat their fill.

__ 10 pts.

At the Beach

Learning about field techniques that scientists use will help you understand the beach, that special place where land meets the sea. Remember to be careful, and have an adult with you when doing these activities. Please return all living creatures to their habitat.

Making the Beach Log

A log is a scientific diary where you record information and observations. To make your beach log you can either buy a small notebook or attach a colorful cover to notebook paper.

On the cover of your log you will want to include your name, the location of the beach you will be studying, and the date.

On the first page of your log include the beach type, (rocky, sandy, etc.). Note the time of high and low tide and the time of sunrise and sunset. You can check the local newspaper for this information.

Make a sketch of the beach on the next page. Now you are ready to start exploring.

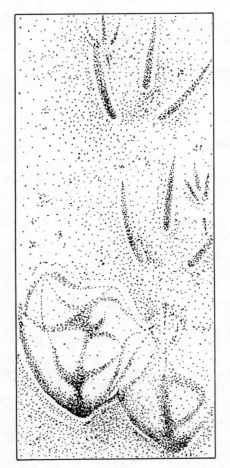

Field Techniques

FOOTPRINTS: An easy way to find out who uses a beach is to look for different kinds of footprints in the sand. Note in your log how many different kinds of prints you see. Draw examples of footprints in your log. You may see prints from birds, small mammals, worms, insects, people, or crabs.

CHICKEN NECKING: A good way to attract crabs is with an old chicken neck tied to a string. Leave it in a shallow area where a stream or marsh meets the ocean. After half an hour or so raise the neck slowly. Did you catch a crab? Did it catch you? Draw a picture of the crab in your log and then put it back in the water.

TIDEPOOLS: Tidepools are full of wonderful animals and plants. Find a safe place to sit and observe the different snails, crabs, seaweed and barnacles that live in the tidepool. List the things you saw and sketch your favorite tidepool creature in your log.

LOG ROLLING: Insects and reptiles live under logs in order to get away from the hot sun and to feed on decaying organic matter. If you see a log on the beach, turn it over by lifting the side farthest from you and lifting it quickly. What do you see? Sketch examples in your log. Return the log.

BEACH COMBING: Make a collection of the treasures that you find as you walk along the beach. How many different kinds of shells can you find? How many shells are round, fan shaped, oval, crescent shaped? Can you find egg cases, fish bones or drift wood? Glue your collection on a piece of cardboard. Use a seashore guide or shell book to help you label your collection.

BIRD WATCHING: Bird watching is a skill which many people enjoy for a lifetime. The easiest way to see birds is to watch them nesting, roosting or feeding. The best time to bird watch is early morning or late afternoon and evening. Observe the shape of the bird's body, beak, and feet. Draw the birds you have seen in your log.

SEINING: Only seine with an adult in very calm waters. Seining is one of the best ways to find out about what lives in the water around you. You will need a net, weighted on one side. Take the net into the water until you are waist deep. Drop the weighted end to the bottom and form an arc with your partner. Walk to shore with the net between you. When you get into shallow water tip the net horizontally so that it will hold your catch. Study your catch but there is no need to kill these sea creatures. Return the animals to the sea and collect your net.

CLAMMING: To determine the number of clams in a certain area, conduct a population census using this method: Using an old hula hoop or rope, place it on the sand at low tide or just before. Dig with your hands, carefully, to avoid sharp shells and glass. When you have found all the clams you can, note the number in your log and try another area. When you have done this six to ten times you can estimate the average clam population for that area by adding the total number of clams and dividing by the total number of digs.

People and the Sea

Do you remember returning to your childhood neighborhood and discovering with surprise that your "huge" backyard was in fact rather small?

Many of us are now realizing that the huge ocean is really not as vast as we once thought. Scientists are discovering industrial chemicals dumped off the east coast of the United States in the waters off the coast of Europe. People walking the beaches of Florida are finding garbage that was carelessly thrown in the ocean by sailors miles off shore. Hawaiian monk seals rest on isolated beaches in the Pacific Ocean that are littered with glass bottles.

Like the vast ocean, many animal populations seemed too plentiful to destroy. In the past, man thoughtlessly hunted whales, seals and sea turtles without concern for the survival of the species. As you know, we have made a drastic reduction in the populations of these marine animals as well as many others. How tragic that the topic for many reports by school children concerns endangered species.

But the message that species are endangered and that the ocean is used as a dumping ground is not new. What is new is the energy that many people are using to stop the destruction of the marine environment and its creatures. People can make a difference in deciding whether the damage continues or stops. What common concern could a dancer, a filmmaker, an explorer and a marine biologist share? After reading their quotes on the following pages you'll know.

We can all take an active part to insure that our ocean planet remains beautiful and rich with resources for generations to come. People do make a difference.

Activities in This Chapter:

Here's What They Say
Read how four people who love the sea have made it a part of their lives.

SEALAB
Aquanaut Scott Carpenter describes his experience working underwater on the ocean floor.

A Deep Sea Tale
It is time for you to make the news. Create a short story about YOUR ocean dive.

In the News
Four ways to get involved with the news.

Identify the Sea Animals
Visit an underwater classroom for kids in Florida.

Oil Spill Clean-up
Help clean up an oil spill using several different methods.

Be a Beach Buddy and a Data Collector
Join the "Beach Buddies" who helped clean the Texas beaches by finding trash on the beach and recording your data.

"Entanglement" in the ocean
Complete the math problems that will inform you of a dangerous situation for marine animals. A problem that you might be able to help solve!

Protecting the Beach
Learn how you can help keep the beach a clean, safe place for people and animals.

Here's What They Say:

From Dr. Eugenie Clark:

When I was nine years old I became interested in sharks and underwater creatures. I loved to visit the New York Aquarium and I would ask my mother to take me there again and again. I was fascinated by the mysterious-looking tank at the back. The green misty water seemed to go on and on. I put my face close to the glass and pretended that I was walking on the bottom of the sea. I would watch the big shark swimming and turning, never resting its long graceful body. I thought someday I'll swim with sharks too. I wish all children could visit an aquarium and develop their own ideas about sea creatures.

Dr. Eugenie Clark is a professor of zoology at the University of Maryland. She is well known for her work with sharks. As a marine biologist she lectures, writes books and articles and loves to dive.

From Captain Cousteau:

Many years ago, before the aqualung, I used to dream a beautiful dream. I was flying in my dream, weightless and free, dipping and soaring and floating. It was a very happy feeling. When I started to dive on scuba under the surface of the sea, my dream stopped. Why? Because I was living my dream, wide awake.

I have many waking dreams, though, things I try hard to accomplish. One of these dreams involves dolphins, and I would like to tell you why.

When dolphins are threatened by an animal of greater strength and size (a large shark, for instance), they come together. A pack of dolphins will suddenly form a tight group, dive below the shark, and drive their blunt noses into its belly, one after another. The shark is defeated by intelligence. The dolphins save themselves by joining together to do what they must.

You and I know we must save the health of our water planet and all creatures on Earth. My dream is that, like dolphins, we can intelligently join together and work together to save our planet and ourselves. You need information. Come learn with us—remember what you learn, and play outdoors and in the sea and among yourselves. You are like dolphins—playful, curious, intelligent, but with dreams of your own. I hope your dreams will all be as beautiful as mine and will all come true.

Captain Cousteau is an explorer, environmentalist, film maker, writer and founder of the Cousteau Society.

From Martita Kingsley Goshen:

I love the ocean because it is the source of all life, all movement. I have been a dancer for some twenty years and the world of the ocean, the sky, the Earth are full of treasures that I love to dance about and most importantly, that I want to protect from man's greed. Extinct is forever. We all have to care.

Martita Kingsley Goshen is a professional dancer and founder of Earthworks, Inc.

From Stanton A. Waterman:

When I started commercial diving thirty years ago, spearfishing was the big thing among sport divers. Man the hunter predominated the new environment. Popular diving areas in the Bahamas and Caribbean were soon speared out. Thirty years later the sport has come of age, and so have the divers. A natural evolution for recreational divers sees their interest change from hunting and destruction to observation and preservation. Today photography dominates the sport.

An educated diving public is now sensitive to the fragility of the marine environment. The future looks somewhat brighter for both the sea and for mankind.

Stan Waterman has produced and directed more than 50 films, including "Blue Water, White Death" and "The Deep." He has won an Emmy award for cinematography.

What do YOU think?

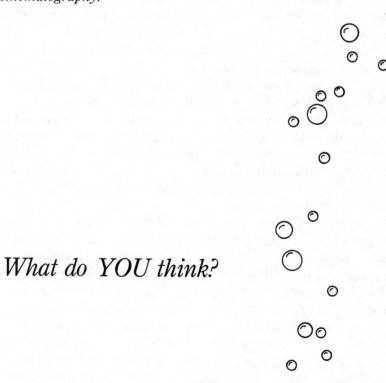

SEALAB
By Scott Carpenter, Aquanaut

My name is Scott Carpenter. I lived on the ocean floor for thirty days in a steel capsule called SEALAB II. In 1965, I was an aquanaut for the U.S. Navy's Man-In-The-Sea program. My work along with the other men who lived in SEALAB 205 feet below the surface was part of an experiment to see if people could live and work for long periods of time in the ocean. This project was a success and a great adventure for me.

My home for thirty days rested on the floor of the Pacific Ocean off the coast of California in very cold water. The other aquanauts and I nicknamed SEALAB II "The Tiltin' Hilton" because its position on the floor of the ocean was slightly tipped. SEALAB looked like a railroad car without any wheels. It was 57 feet long and 12 feet in diameter and just like your house it had a kitchen, bathroom, beds and closets. It even had windows that we could look out of and watch fish looking in at us.

The air in SEALAB was not like the air that we breathe on land. A special mix of helium, nitrogen and a little oxygen kept us alive under pressure seven times greater than on land. The helium made our voices much higher than normal, and when we spoke to each other we sounded like Donald Duck. This voice change made us laugh.

My time in SEALAB was spent eating, sleeping, talking to the other team members and preparing for dives outside the capsule. Because the water was so cold we wore electrically heated suits for the dives. Even with these suits we could only spend about one hour in the water before returning to SEALAB for a shower and hot food. The team members and I set up an underwater weather station to measure temperatures and currents and did marine experiments such as tagging fish, collecting rock samples, and taking pictures of sea creatures. During one of my dives, I was stung by a scorpion fish. This painful sting lasted for about two days, but I was treated by a doctor who was part of the SEALAB team. Being weightless and working in the water made me very tired and hungry. Just keeping warm in the cold water took a great deal of energy. I would return to SEALAB shaking from the cold, and ready to eat. We all ate lots of snacks and drank lots of juice. Fruits and vegetables were sent down to us every day from the men on the command vessel above.

Our only regular visitor was a trained porpoise named "Tuffy" who delivered our mail and some supplies. If any of our divers got lost in the dark water Tuffy could easily find him and lead him back to SEALAB with his built-in sonar.

During my underwater stay medical tests were always being taken to see if my body was going through any major changes. Blood, urine, saliva, throat, nose and ear tests were taken. After the thirty days underwater, more tests were taken back on land. I did not have any problems other than minor head and ear aches. With a few changes in the atmosphere inside SEALAB, the number of head and ear aches were reduced for other divers who lived in SEALAB after I returned to land.

My team and I returned to the surface in an "elevator" that had the same mix of gases that we had been breathing in SEALAB. We were then transferred into a deck decompression chamber where we spent about 31 hours breathing a mixture of gases that gradually reached the mixture and pressure of the air we normally breathe on land. If decompression is not done properly, divers develop a painful and sometimes fatal reaction called the bends.

When I finally was allowed to leave the decompression chamber I felt tired, but very happy and proud of all the work we had done. The bottom of the sea holds minerals and oil that are important resources for people. Getting food from the ocean is going to be very important as the world's population continues to increase. If we utilize wisely the resources of the sea we can help people on land. The work done with Project SEALAB showed that it is possible for people to live and do work on the ocean floor. Maybe someday you too will have this chance.

A Deep Sea Tale...

Reported by _____ ,
Great Underwater Explorer

Write a short story about your dive deep in the ocean. Describe what you saw, how you felt, and tell about your discovery.

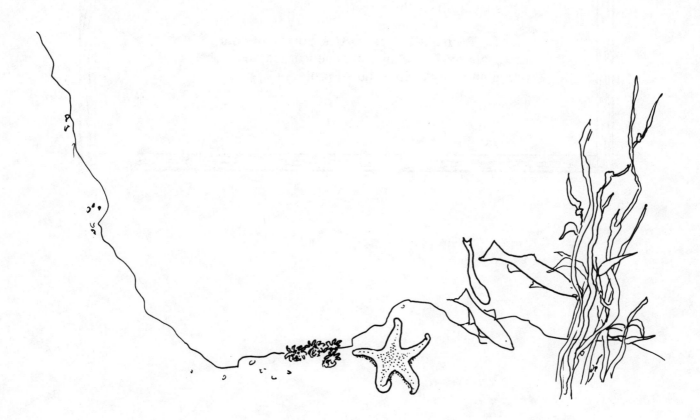

In the News

OCEAN EVENTS

1. Make an "OCEAN EVENTS" bulletin board. Check the newspapers each day for news about the ocean environment. Cut out the articles and post them on the board.

2. Pretend that you are a journalist. Write a story about a disaster that has hit a beach, such as a hurricane, or an oil spill. Describe what happened to the beach, the animals and the people.

3. Plan a news conference in your classroom. Invite a scientist, an environmentalist and a fisherman to come to your classroom and talk about the marine environment. Write a story for your school newspaper about their visit.

4. Write a letter to the editor of your local newspaper about what you have learned about the ocean and why people should protect it.

In the News

OCEAN EVENTS

Identify the Sea Animals

As the students look out the porthole of their underwater classroom, they see many different animals. See how many you know, from the description on this page.

Put the correct number of the description in the blank under the animal. Color the underwater classroom.

1. **Crab**
   I have a thick, heavy shell and move sideways over the sand. My pincers can hurt!

2. **Octopus**
   I have many arms called tentacles and can swim backwards. Sometimes my body changes color to hide me from my enemies.

3. **Sea Urchin**
   My spines are sharp. Don't touch me! People in Japan like to eat me.

4. **Barracuda**
   I swim very fast and have large razor-sharp teeth.

5. **Starfish**
   I have five arms which I use for eating and swimming. My "skin" is covered in tiny spines.

6. **Sand Dollar**
   My outer body is hard, flat and very delicate. I like to live on the bottom of the ocean.

7. **Brittle Star**
   I have long, thin arms called tentacles. I live in the soft mud. The starfish is my relative.

8. **Sea Anemone**
   My soft body can be pink, purple and many other colors. Look at my tentacles wave in the water.

The underwater classroom on the next page is a 22 ton metal laboratory, 8 feet wide and 16 feet long in the Atlantic Ocean near Key Largo, Florida.

High School students interested in marine science live in this undersea lab for 24 hours. These young aquanauts learn about the ocean in a very unique way.

Marine Resources Underwater Classroom

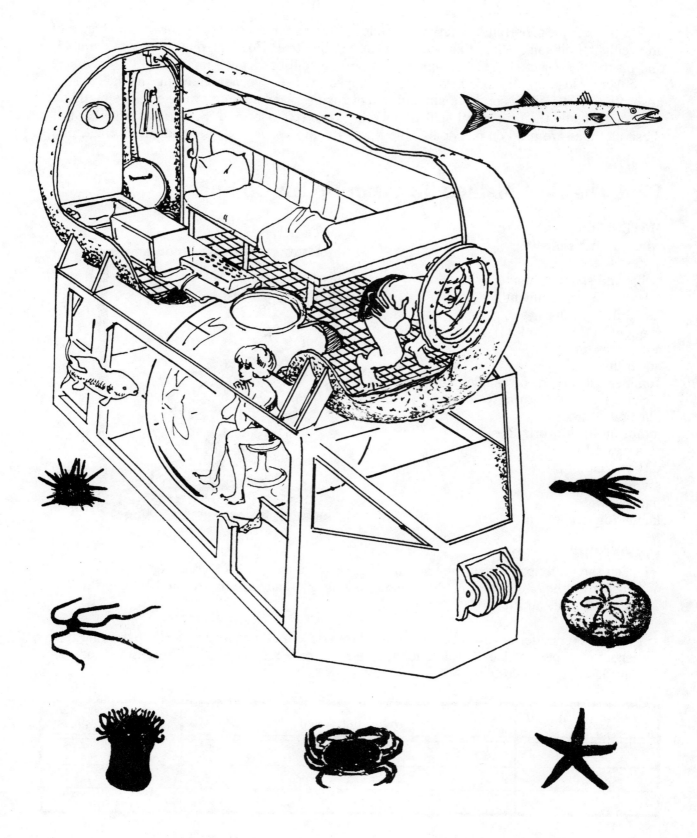

Courtesy of Marine Resources Development Foundation

Oil Spill Clean-up

In this age of supertankers ferrying crude oil across the seas, there is always a chance of an accidental oil spill. When this occurs, what can be done? How can one protect the animal and plant life subjected to the oil spill? How can the spill be cleaned up?

Several clean-up methods have been developed. These involve containing the spill, adsorption of the oil, absorption, skimming, coagulating, and sinking of the oil. The method used depends on the type of oil spilled and where the spill occurred. Sometimes several of these methods are used on one spill. This activity compares various methods used in cleaning up an oil spill.

Find The Best Method To Clean Up An Oil Spill

MATERIALS

white plastic sinks
water
twigs and string to make a
  boom for containment
liquid detergent
sponge
soda straws
aquarium net
commercial sorbent (available from
  State Dept. of Natural Resources)
plastic trash bag
motor oil (used works best)
straw (not hay)
dirt or sand
styrofoam pieces
paper towels
kaolin (diatomous earth)

PROCEDURES

1. Tell the participants that they are an EPA (Environmental Protection Agency) team rushed to the site of a grounded tanker spilling oil. They are to use the best possible method to clean it up.

2. Divide the students into teams to study the various methods available. Prepare a large sheet of paper or blackboard as follows to record the results of the different methods used:

Method	What happened	Rating as to effectiveness (1-5)

Courtesy of Smithsonian Environmental Research Center

3. Give the participants a white basin to fill with water and to which they add oil to create their own oil spill. If necessary, after each method is tried, more oil may be added. The used oily materials are to be placed into the plastic garbage bag. Tilt the sinks to make "waves." Observe to see if this changes the effectiveness of each clean-up method.

4. Some methods to try and rate as to their effectiveness.
   a) Straw—place on oil and remove
   b) Paper towel—place on oil and remove
   c) Styrofoam pieces—place on oil and remove
   d) Boom of twigs tied together—pulled across the spill, or place around spill to contain it
   e) Soda straw—blow bubbles under oil (a ring of bubbles will contain spill)
   f) Detergent—add a drop to spill to disperse oil.
   g) Sand sprinkled on surface of oil water
   h) Kaolin sprinkled on surface of oil water
   i) Commercial sorbent sprinkled on surface of oil water
   j) Aquarium net—scoop up oil
   k) Any additional methods suggested by participants

5. Using any one or all of the methods suggested, have the participants clean up the oil spill in their sink.

QUESTIONS
1. What method appeared to work best? Why?
2. Would the same method work for every spill?
3. Does the method have any bad effects on the environment?
4. How could an oil spill be prevented from spreading?
5. Who should be responsible for cleaning up a spill?
6. How might oil spills be prevented?

Courtesy of Smithsonian Environmental Research Center

Be a Beach Buddy

One Saturday in September 1986, 2770 people in Texas helped to clean their beaches. Men, women, and children collected 124 tons of trash in 3 hours. Because of strong currents in the Gulf of Mexico, trash that is thrown off boats into the water will wash up on Texas beaches. Some trash also comes from careless beach users. Be a Beach Buddy and, first, color the trash using the colors listed below. Next, count the beach trash and list your numbers on the data card on the next page.

Gloves	. . . . . . red
Oil drums	. . . . yellow
Hard hats	. . . . blue
Jugs	. . . . orange
Ropes	. . . . purple
Plants	. . . . green

Be a Data Collector

The volunteers in Texas kept track of what they found on data cards. Data is a word scientists use to mean information. Use the data card below to count the trash you find in the picture on the opposite page. Use tick marks in groups of 5, like this: ╫╫

DATA CARD		
Kind of Trash	How Many?	TOTAL
Plastic Jugs		
Hard Hats		
Gloves		
Ropes		
*55 Gallon Drums		

*These drums often contain dangerous chemicals. If you see one on the beach *DO NOT* go near it.

During the 1986 Texas Beach Clean-up, Beach Buddies found:

5,308	milk jugs
127	hard hats
1,030	gloves
6,367	ropes
215	metal drums

Collecting data during beach cleanups is very important. The types and amounts of trash found on the beach can tell us where the trash is coming from, and can enable scientists and others to develop solutions to the marine debris problem.

Entanglement in the Ocean

All kinds of things are being dumped into the ocean off of boats and from the shore. Many of these products, including ropes, picnic items, fishing line, hardhats and more, are made of a substance that does not rot or decay for a long, long time. Thousands of ocean animals are getting caught in these products. When an animal gets caught and trapped by these materials, it is called "entanglement." Do the math problems and figure out what the sea lion's head is entangled in. It is the same substance that so many products are made of that end up floating in the ocean.

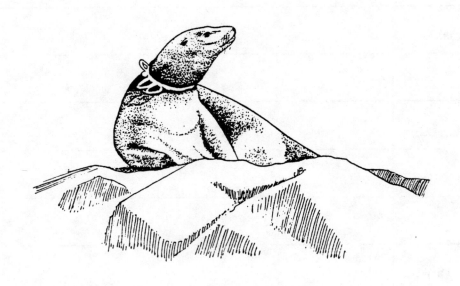

(9×6)	(12×4)	(7×10)	(3×8)	(8×9)	(11×5)	(14×2)

Now that you have solved the math problems, translate the mystery code from numbers to letters to figure out what the sea lion is entangled in:

___ ___ ___ ___ ___ ___ ___

A = 70	I = 55	Q = 22
B = 16	J = 75	R = 59
C = 28	K = 21	S = 24
D = 12	L = 48	T = 72
E = 105	M = 32	U = 63
F = 42	N = 1	V = 41
G = 11	O = 9	W = 50
H = 6	P = 54	X = 2

Protecting the Beach

While exploring the beach you may have noticed litter in the area. Some people are not careful about leaving the beach as clean as when they arrived. You can help make your beach a nice, safe place for people and animals with these simple suggestions.

- Always take a trash bag with you and pick up any trash you see. Plastic "six-pack" holders are especially dangerous because birds and other animals get them caught around their necks.

- Every year hundreds of marine animals get caught in fishing net fragments. Some animals die while trying to swim free of the nets. Many animals suffer by having net pieces caught tightly around their necks. If you see a piece of net on the beach, please pick it up and dispose of it properly.

- If you are on a beach where sea turtles nest there are several things you can do to help these endangered animals.
  —Avoid disturbing a turtle that is crawling to or from the ocean.
  —Avoid crowding around her, snapping flash photos, or shining lights into her eyes.
  —Discourage other people from bothering the turtle.
  —Do not disturb the sand anywhere near a sea turtle nest.
  —Do not go near areas that are posted as nesting areas. You may crush the buried eggs.

- Plastic bags in the ocean are often mistakenly eaten by animals who think they are food. Many animals die from eating plastic bags. Dispose of plastic bags carefully.

CHAPTER 8

Reference

  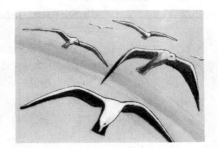

Vocabulary List

Adaptation . . . . unique characteristic that helps an animal survive in its habitat.

Arctic Ocean . . . . surrounds the North Pole. It is the smallest ocean.

Atlantic Ocean . . . . . the second largest ocean.

Baleen . . . . sheets of fringed horny materials used for feeding instead of teeth by some kinds of whales.

Baleen whale . . . . whales that sift planktonic organisms from the water using their baleen plate. Blue whales are the largest of the baleen whales.

Blowhole . . . . a nostril on the top of the head of a cetacean used for breathing.

Blubber . . . . a thick fatty layer of tissue for keeping warm found in most marine mammals.

Breaching . . . . a word used to describe how whales leap out of the water.

Camouflage . . . . blending into the surroundings for protection.

Carnivore . . . . a meat eater.

Cetaceans . . . . the group of marine mammals consisting of whales and dolphins.

Climate . . . . the weather typical to an area including temperature, precipitation and wind.

Consumer . . . . animals that feed on plants and animals.

Continental shelf . . . the undersea ledge that forms the rim of a continent.

Continental slope . . . the steep slope between the continental shelf and the ocean floor.

Crest . . . . the top of a wave.

Current . . . . a body of water that flows through the sea.

Density . . . . the amount of something per unit measure.

Diatom . . . . single-celled plant that floats near the surface of the sea and forms the base of the food pyramid on which all animal life depends directly or indirectly.

Echolocation . . . . the emission of sound waves under water by marine mammals. The returning sound wave helps the animals identify the size and location of an object.

Ecology . . . . the relationship between plants and animals and their environment.

Ecosystem . . . . all the living organisms and the physical features within a specific area.

Environment . . . . . . our surroundings, including all of the living and non-living parts.

Estuary . . . . a semi-enclosed body of water in which fresh water combines with salt water.

Evaporation . . . . the process of a liquid changing into a vapor. The sun's heat evaporates water in the liquid state to water vapor.

Filter feeders . . . . animals that eat by collecting small particles of food from the water. Oysters are filter feeders.

First-order consumer . . . . consumers which feed on the energy stored by producers. The plant feeders.

Fish . . . . a coldblooded animal with a backbone which lives in water and breathes with gills.

Fluke . . . . a whale's tail.

Food chain . . . . a series of plants and animals linked by their feeding relationships.

Food web . . . . food chains which overlap and interconnect.

Gill . . . . the organ for fish to breathe oxygen in the water.

Gyotaku . . . . Japanese fish printing, used for more than a century for recording catches of sportfish.

Habitat . . . . the place where an animal lives.

Herbivore . . . . a plant eater.

Ichthyologist . . . . a person who studies fish.

Indian Ocean . . . . situated east of Africa, it is smaller than the Atlantic and Pacific Oceans.

Invertebrate . . . . an animal with no backbone.

Kelp . . . . any of various large brown seaweeds.

Krill . . . . shrimp-like animals that feed on diatoms and live in the waters near Antarctica. Fish, birds, and mammals eat krill.

Lungs . . . . used by marine mammals, like all mammals, to breathe.

Mammal . . . . warmblooded animal with a backbone that gives birth to live young and produces milk to feed its newborn.

Mammary glands . . . structures in female mammals that produce milk to feed their young.

Mammologist . . . . . . a person who studies mammals.

Melon . . . . a mass of fatty tissue on a dolphin's forehead through which sounds are projected.

Microscopic . . . . very small. Can only be seen with a microscope.

Neap tides . . . . tides during the half moon that are not as great as Spring tides.

Ocean . . . . the body of salt water that covers over 70% of the Earth's surface.

Pacific Ocean . . . . the largest and deepest ocean.

Photosynthesis . . . . . process in which green plants trap the sun's energy and produce food.

Phytoplankton . . . . . microscopic plants which drift and float in the sea, necessary for life in the sea.

Pinnipeds . . . . category of marine mammals that includes seals, sea lions and walruses.

Plankton . . . . small organisms which are not strong swimmers and drift and float with the waves; plants and animals.

Pods . . . . a small social group or family of cetaceans.

Predator . . . . an animal that captures and eats other animals.

Prey . . . . an animal that is eaten by other animals.

Producer . . . . plant life which, through photosynthesis, traps the sun's energy and produces food for animals.

Seal . . . . a pinniped that propels itself with its hind flippers and is generally awkward on land.

Sea Lion . . . . a pinniped that propels itself with its front flippers and is very agile on land.

Second-Order Consumer . . . . consumers which feed on first order consumers.

Sonar . . . . mechanical echolocation device humans use involving the sending and receiving of sound waves for identification purposes.

Spring tides . . . . extra-high high tides and extra-low low tides occurring as the sun and moon line up and pull upon the Earth together.

Symbiosis . . . . two kinds of animals living together for survival.

Tide . . . . the rise and fall of the ocean caused by the gravitational pull of the moon and sun.

Tidepool . . . . an area among the rocky shores that is covered by water during the high tide and exposed to the air when the tide is low. Crabs, sea stars, and mussels are a few of the animals that live in this environment.

Trench . . . . a deep gash or valley in the ocean floor.

Trough . . . . the lowest point in a wave between the crests.

Vertebrate . . . . an animal with a backbone.

Volcano . . . . a vent in the Earth's crust through which hot, melted rock and gases are ejected.

Water cycle . . . . the movement of water from sky to earth and back to sky.

Wavelength . . . . the distance between crests of a wave.

Whale . . . . a marine mammal.

Zooplankton . . . . small animals which drift in the sea.

Book List

Asimov, Isaac. *How Did We Find Out About Life in the Deep Sea?* New York: Avon Books, 1982.

Austin, Elizabeth S. *Penguins: The Birds with Flippers*. New York: Random House, 1968.

Beck, Horace. *Folklore and the Sea*. Middletown, CT: Wesleyan University Press, 1973.

Berrill, N. J., and Jacquelyn Berrill. *1001 Questions Answered About the Seashore*. New York: Dover Publications, Inc., 1957.

Blassingame, Wyatt. *Wonders of the Turtle World*. New York: Dodd, Mead, and Co., 1976.

Brindze, Ruth. *The Rise and Fall of the Seas: The Story of Tides*. New York: Harcourt Brace Jovanovich, 1964.

Brown, Joseph E. *Wonders of Seals and Sea Lions*. New York: Dodd, Mead, and Co., 1976.

Brown, Louise C. *Elephant Seals*. New York: Dodd, Mead, and Co., 1979.

Burton, Robert. *Seals*. New York: McGraw-Hill, 1979.

Campbell, Elizabeth A. *Fins and Tails: A Story of Strange Fish*. Boston: Little, Brown and Co., 1963.

Carr, Archie F. *So Excellent A Fishe: A Natural History of Sea Turtles*. New York: Natural History Press, 1967.

————. *The Windward Road*. Gainesville: University Press of Florida, 1979.

Carrighar, Sally. *The Twilight Seas: A Blue Whale's Journey*. New York: Ballantine Books, 1976.

Carson, Rachel L. *The Edge of the Sea*. Boston: Houghton Mifflin Co., 1955.

————. *The Sea Around Us*. New York: Oxford University Press, 1950.

Clemons, Elizabeth. *Waves, Tides and Currents*. New York: Alfred A. Knopf, 1967.

Conklin, Gladys. *Journey of the Gray Whales*. New York: Holiday House, 1974.

Coulombe, Deborah. *The Seaside Naturalist:* A Guide to Nature at the Seashore. Englewood Cliffs, N.J.: Prectice-Hall, 1984.

Curtsinger, William R., and Kenneth Brower. *Wake of the Whale*. New York: E. P. Dutton, 1979.

Ellis, Richard. *The Book of Whales*. New York: Alfred A. Knopf, 1980.

Goodridge, Harry. *A Seal Called Andre*. New York: Warner Books, 1975.

Griggs, Tamar. *There's a Sound in the Sea: A Child's Eye View of the Whale*. Oakland: Scrimshaw Press, 1975.

Groves, Donald. *The Oceans: A Book of Questions and Answers*. New York: John Wiley & Sons, 1989.

Hiser, Iona S. *The Seals*. Austin: Steck-Vaughn Co., 1975.

Hogner, Dorothy C. *Sea Mammals*. New York: Harper and Row, 1979.

Kelly, John E., Scott Mercer, and Steve Wolf. *The Great Whale Book*. Washington: Center for Environmental Education, 1981.

Lambert, David. *The Oceans*. New York: The Bookwright Press, 1984.

Lewin, Ted. *World Within a World—The Pribilofs*. New York: Dodd, Mead, and Co., 1980.

McGovern, Ann. *Shark Lady, True Adventures of Eugenie Clark*. New York: Scholastic Book Services, 1978.

O'Dell, Scott. *Island of the Blue Dolphin*. New York: Dell Publishing Co., 1960.

O'Hara, Kathryn J. et al. *Citizens Guide to Plastic in the Ocean: More than a Litter Problem*. Washington: Center for Marine Conservation, 1988.

Pringle, Lawrence. *Chains, Webs, and Pyramids*. New York: Thomas Y. Crowell Co., 1975.

Rabinowich, Ellen. *Seals, Sea Lions, and Walruses*. New York: Franklin Watts, 1980.

Riedman, Sarah R., and Ross Witham. *Turtles: Extinction or Survival?* New York: Abelard-Schuman, 1974.

Selsam, Millicente, and Joyce Hunt. *A First Look at Whales*. New York: Walker and Co., 1980.

Shannon, Terry, and Charles Paysant. *Project SEALAB, The Story of the United States Navy's Man-in-the-Sea Program*. San Carlos, CA: Golden Gate Junior Press, 1966.

Weyl, Peter. *Oceanography: An Introduction to the Marine Environment*. New York: John Wiley and Sons, 1970.

Zim, Herbert. *The Waves*. New York: William Morrow and Co., 1967.

Answers to Activities

Chapter 1
Dive In

World Map to Color and Label

The Largest Ocean is the Pacific Ocean

The Water Cycle

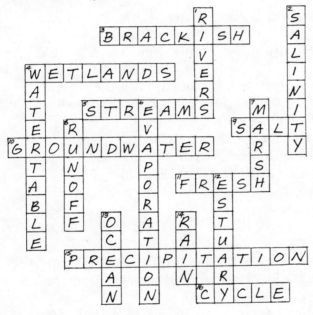

The Ocean Floor

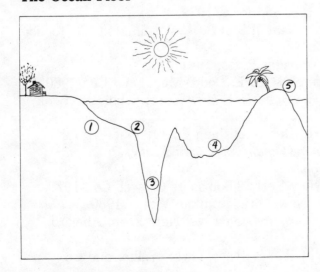

Gee Whiz Ocean Quiz

1. **True**. The oceans cover about 133 million square miles or an area 37 times the size of the United States.

2. **200,000 years**.

3. **True**. The oceans contain about 97 percent of all the water on Earth with most of the remainder being locked up in the polar ice caps.

4. **False**. A cubic mile of sea water weighs about 4.7 billion tons and contains about 165 millions tons of chlorine, sodium, magnesium, carbon, nitrogen, phosphorus, arsenic, silver, and gold. For comparison, the Statue of Liberty weighs 225 tons.

5. **500**.

6. **True**.

7. **12,300 feet**. If the Earth's surface were smooth, with no mountain peaks or ocean basins, it would be completely covered with water to a depth of 12,000 feet.

8. **False**. The peak would be covered by about 8,000 feet of water.

9. **False**. For instance, off our coasts are submarine canyons whose walls may be as high as 14,000 feet. These canyons may stretch for 200 miles to the deep ocean plain.

10. The average temperature of the oceans is about **38 degrees** Fahrenheit.

11. **False**. It is estimated that nine out of every ten organisms on Earth live in the oceans.

12. **True**. Some squid have the largest eye in nature—over 15 inches in diameter.

13. The **Pacific**, whose average depth is 13,200 feet. The average depth of the Atlantic Ocean is 12,880 feet.

14. **Animals**. Barrel sponges may grow large enough to hold two people and filter hundreds of gallons of water each day from which they strain their food.

15. **The blue whale**, which may attain a length of over 100 feet.

16. **False**. A female blue crab may release over one million eggs into the water during spawning season.

17. The United States has a tidal shoreline of more than **88,000 miles** or more than three times the circumference of the Earth.

18. **True**. More than 120 million Americans live within 50 miles of the coast. By 1990, 75 percent of the U.S. population will live in this area.

19. **True**. In an average year, about 20 million of us go ocean fishing, spending almost $4 billion on equipment, food and drink, lodging and transportation.

20. **False**. About 70 percent of commercially valuable fish spend a significant part of their lives in estuaries and wetlands.

21. **False**. The "red tides" which sometimes turn our coastal waters deadly for fish and other animals are the result of blooms of tiny plants called dinoflagellates. Two pints of water may contain as many as half a million of these tiny plants during a "bloom."

22. **False**: About 17,000 years ago, the sea level was about 400 feet lower than at the present. About 250 million years ago the sea level was high enough that large barrier reefs flourished in west Texas. About 400 million years ago the sea level was so high that vast coral reefs lay in a belt across what is now called Indiana, Illinois, and Wisconsin.

23. **True**. A sperm whale has large cone shaped teeth on its lower jaw that are used for grabbing and holding its prey.

24. **True**. Emperor penguins do incubate their eggs on their feet.

25. **True**. Penguins feed only in the ocean.

26. **True**: A new born baby blue whale weighs over 4000 pounds.

27. **True**: An adult emperor penguin measures four feet from beak to tail.

28. **False**: The blue sea is caused by the scattering of sunlight by tiny particles suspended in water. Blue light being of short wave length is scattered more effectively than light of longer wave lengths. Not all sea water is blue. Some is green, brown or brownish red.

29. **False**. The saltiness of the oceans is due to a slow process which has been going on for hundreds of millions of years. It is believed that the primeval seas were initially salty having dissolved salts from the rocks underlying their basins. The breaking up of rocks on land has added to the salts of the sea.

30. **True**. The average thickness of the Arctic ice pack is about 9 to 10 feet, although in some areas it is 65 feet thick.

Chapter 2
Currents and Weather

Ocean Currents

Experiment 1: Salinity Currents—Interpretation

1. Salt water is heavier. The colored salty water sank into the clear fresh water in experimental set up "a."

2. Since river water is fresh, it floats on top of the salt water until waves and currents cause the two to mix.

3. Freddy was fishing where the fresh water was standing in a layer above the salt water. Near the surface the water was the lighter river water, near the bottom the water was the more dense sea water.

Experiment 2: Temperature Currents—Interpretation

1. Warm water is lighter (lower density) than cool water. The warm, colored water remained in the upper flask in experimental set up "a."

2. Most heating occurs at the surface.

3. Most dilution of sea water occurs at the surface.

4. It is easier for a human to swim in salt water. The salt water makes the person more bouyant. Salt water is more dense and the same volume displaced by the person will weigh more, the person floats more easily.

5. It is easier for a human to swim in cool water. The person displaces the same volume but since the water is cooler and more dense it weighs more and the person floats more readily. A word of warning may be in order here. While a person will float more readily in cool water, the chance of excessive body heat loss increases. Cold water can lead to hypothermia. You may wish to discuss this so that your students use caution when experimenting on their own.

Tide Mobile

1. Spring Tides

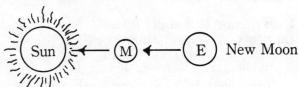

New Moon

2. Neap Tides

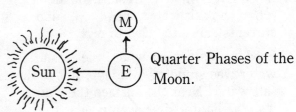

Quarter Phases of the Moon.

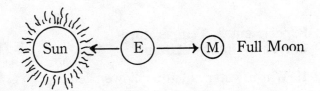

Full Moon

1. Earth, Moon and Sun are in a straight line during Spring Tides.
2. Earth, Moon, and Sun are at right angles to each other during Neap Tides.

The Ocean? No Sweat!

1. Near the coast.

2. Inland.

3. Water does not lose heat or gain heat as fast as the land. Therefore, a water mass tends to cool land during the day and heat it during the night. Temperatures do not reach the extremes they would at a site far from a water mass.

Chapter 3
Who's Who: Animals in the Ocean

Whales and Fish

Whales
Are warm blooded
Give birth to live young
Come to surface for air
Breathe through their lungs

Fish
Are cold blooded
Usually lay eggs
Breathe oxygen dissolved in water
Breathe with their gills

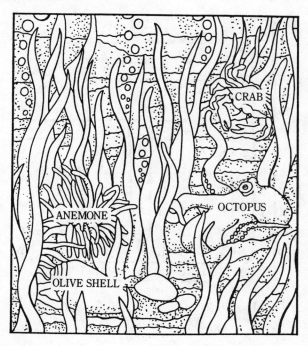

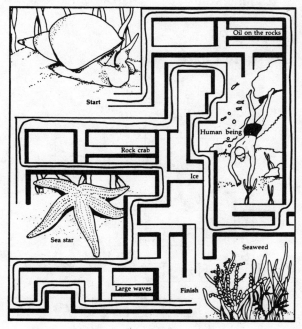

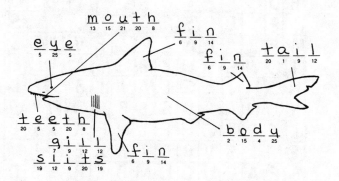

A Whale of a Tail

mammals
lungs
blowholes
blubber
aquatic
baleen
toothed
toothed
teeth

baleen
krill
intelligent
echolocation
breaching
pod
Dolphins are
toothed whales.

Marine Mammal Crossword Puzzle

(crossword grid with answers: SONAR, PINNIPEDS, PODS, BLUBBER, HERBIVORE, SEALION, MAMMARYGLANDS, EARFLAP, TUSK, WHISKERS, BLOWHOLE, PLANKTON, CARNIVORE, SEA OTTER, CETACEAN, FLIPPER, BREACHING, FLUKES, BALEEN, MELON, TRAINED, SANDS)

Find Me

CRAB

ANEMONE

OCTOPUS

OLIVE SHELL

Chapter 4

Food Chains...Come and Eat!

Maze

Oil on the rocks

Start

Human being

Rock crab

Ice

Sea star

Seaweed

Large waves   Finish

Sherlock Shark

m o u t h
13 15 21 20 8

e y e
5 25 5

f i n
6 9 14

f i n
6 9 14

t a i l
20 1 9 12

t e e t h
20 5 5 20 8

b o d y
2 15 4 25

g i l l
7 9 12 12

s l i t s
19 12 9 20 19

f i n
6 9 14

What kind of animal is a shark? f i s h
6 9 19 8

Find-a-Word

```
P L A N K T O N L T T Y P E
H R Z P R O D U C E R R G M
Y F O O D C H A I N O V M A
T T O P D Y N M B I L W M K
O P P A E F T F U I O T R E
P P L M I C R O S C O P I C
P L C A E X P W O R X I T E W
L A B N C E R I D Z A R G D I
A R K K T E D W R V X A U O
N T T W R R T E B O H J K L
K O O N R B J B E C S W H O
T J N Y N G R V M O I P F W
O N U T G C O N S U M E R W M
```

B.	1. Plankton		G.	5. Consumer
D.	2. Food Web		C.	6. Food Chain
E.	3. Phytoplankton		H.	7. Zooplankton
A.	4. Producer		I.	8. Microscopic

Sea Food Chain

1. Sun
2. Phytoplankton
3. Zooplankton
4. Herring
5. Bluefish
6. Decomposers

Catching Food
Crossword Puzzle

```
        ²C  ³S  T  E  E  T  H
        A   I           E
        ⁶M  O  O  N      N      ⁵M
        O       ⁷B       S      O
        U       ⁸F  O  O  D     U
        ⁹F  O  O  D     ⁹C  A  T  C  H   T
        L              A       H
   ¹¹E  E  L           ¹²S  P  I  N  E  S
        A   ¹²S                V
   ¹³P  R  E  D  A  T  O  R     E
        T                      ¹⁴B
        ¹⁵F  I  L  T  E  R  F  E  E  D  E  R  S
        ¹⁶C  L  A  W  S
```

Predator—Prey

Killer whale—seal
Sea Cow—sea grass
Sea Star—clam
Tiggerfish—sea urchin
The sea cow is the herbivore.

Chapter 5
Adaptation
Adaptation Code

A. Camouflage
B. Symbiosis
C. Territory
D. Schooling
E. Rheotaxis
F. Attachment

Hawaiian Fish

1. Bandit Fish
2. Goat Fish
3. Stick Fish
4. Squirrel Fish
5. Parrot Fish
6. Surgeon Fish
7. Lion Fish
8. Butterfly Fish
9. Damsel Fish
10. Angel Fish

Chapter 6
Ecosystems

Tidepool Word Search

```
P T H E R M I T C R A B A R
E I R O C K W E E D Q L N M
R D O S E A U R C H I N E U
I E F E L S C A L L O P M S
W P B A R N A C L E V U O S
I O W S M U Z R G F A H N E
N O H T K Q L A J I B S E L
K U N A P B S B P S O P K S
L X E R O H F L N H K O J L
E M I S V R D T W X E N I M
S E A C U C U M B E R G B D
L Z A R Y D L O B S T E R A
```

Beach Walk

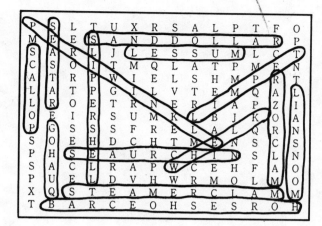

Sea Side Riddles

1. Horseshoe crab
2. Hermit crab
3. Fiddler crab
4. Barnacle

5. Kelp
6. Sea turtle
7. Star fish
8. Pelican

Chapter 7

People and the Sea

Identify the Sea Animals

1. Crab

2. Octopus

3. Sea Urchin

4. Barracuda

5. Starfish

6. Sand Dollar

7. Brittle Star

8. Sea Anemone

Be a Beach Buddy

You should have found 7 plastic jugs, 7 hard hats, 13 gloves, 4 pieces of rope, and 4 drums.

Entanglement in the Ocean

$$\frac{54}{(9 \times 6)} \quad \frac{48}{(12 \times 4)} \quad \frac{70}{(7 \times 10)} \quad \frac{24}{(3 \times 8)} \quad \frac{72}{(8 \times 9)} \quad \frac{55}{(11 \times 5)} \quad \frac{28}{(14 \times 2)}$$

P   L   A   S   T   I   C